Battlegrou

LAD

Colenso/Spion Kop/Thangwane/Tugela

Battleground South Africa

LADYSMITH
Colenso/Spion Kop/Hlangwane/Tugela

Lewis Childs

Series editor
Nigel Cave

LEO COOPER

First published in 1998 by
LEO COOPER
190 Shaftesbury Avenue, London WC2H 8JL
an imprint of
Pen Sword Books Limited
47 Church Street, Barnsley, South Yorkshire S70 2AS

ISBN 0 85052 611 6

A CIP catalogue of this book is available
from the British Library

Printed by Redwood Books Limited
Trowbridge, Wiltshire

*For up-to-date information on other titles produced under the Leo Cooper imprint,
please telephone or write to:*

Pen & Sword Books Ltd, FREEPOST, 47 Church Street
Barnsley, South Yorkshire S70 2AS
Telephone 01226 734222

Front cover illustration: In Rotterdam, at the time of the South African War, there was a theatre called the 'Transvalia'. The walls of the foyer were ornamented by representations of battles of the conflict, and were mainly favourable to the Boers. They were executed on 150mm square tiles but eventually were papered over and lost until the place was restored in the 1960s. They now adorn the walls of the War Museum of the Boer Republics, Bloemfontein and, by kind permission, our front cover is 'Colenso' from that series.

Contents

'One rarely thinks of the way in which horses have no part in deciding when and how they work, but here in this story it strikes forcibly how fearful it would be for them too.' (Attempting to recover the guns at Colenso, page 61).

Introduction by Series Editor

The Boer War, which straddled the last years of the nineteenth and the first years of the twentieth centuries, was of very considerable significance to the evolution of the British Empire and to the development of the British Army. It brought the British face to face with a relatively rare experience in its colonial policing, that is a well armed and motivated white rebellious force, under some inspired generalship. It took some considerable resources to bring the war to a successful conclusion, and the cost in manpower and prestige was considerable. It is to the credit of both sides that the fighting was brought to a conclusion which allowed some dignity for the participants in the conflict, with the British government even compensating the Boers for the farms burned in the dirty war that characterised the last two years of fighting. It even allowed a situation that brought the South Africans into the Great War, their fighting contribution being most graphically shown by their memorial at Delville Wood on the Somme. Jan Smuts, who had fought against the British, was to be a most valued member of Lloyd George's War Cabinet, and played a vital role in the establishment of the Royal Air Force.

The Boer War also showed Britain's weakness when vigorously challenged, and this point would not have been lost on Mahatma Ghandi, who served in South Africa as a stretcher-bearer. The other victims of this war were the native South Africans, whose services both sides pressed into action as labourers and who presumably suffered considerably as a consequence, often as innocent bystanders of the 'white mans' war'. There is little mention of them in the existing record.

The British Army was subjected to a ferocious review of its performance after the war, and this in turn led to the many reforms that were to lead to the highly proficient force that was landed on the continent in 1914 where the army, as so often before and since, was required to punch above its weight. All was not a dismal record of error, failure and incompetence before a well-organised and commanded foe, and a particular bright spot was the effective use of Parson's guns on 27th February 1900, the anniversary of the British defeat at Majuba Hill, 1881.

Lewis Childs' book is the first in the Battleground series to move out of Europe – in fact the first to break away from the Great War. With the hundredth anniversary of these events fast approaching and with the opening of the beautiful and tortured country of South Africa to the foreign traveller, the time seems to be ripe to provide a Battlefield guide to events thousands of miles from the home country, but which were to be of such importance to the capability of a British Expeditionary Force sent to France in 1914 and such a formative experience for many of its commanders.

Nigel Cave
Ely Place, London

Maps

Acknowledgments

I began this book as a novice and feel, as I conclude the writing, that nothing much has altered in that regard! What I have learned, however, is the joy of research and more than that the vast willingness of many people to assist in something that they think may, just may, bring to the public attention a subject dear to their own heart. Or alternatively they see an opportunity to make useful the facts stacked in cardboard boxes and immured in cupboards: facts to do with dead men, often fighting and dying in dead causes, but doing so with dignity and loyalty to vows made. Neither politicians nor captains of commerce come out well, in my view, but soldiers in the field show the most amazing tolerance and dedication.

Curators and Keepers of Archives at several Regimental Museums have been most helpful to me, notably, H.G. Forrester, and then Major G. E. M. Stephens MBE DL, successively Curators of The Royal Inniskilling Fusiliers Regimental Museum: Amanda Moreno, Royal Irish Fusiliers Museum, Armagh: Peter Donnelly at the King's Own Royal Regiment Museum, Lancaster: Major Hallam, the Curator, and his assistant Tony Sprayson at the Lancashire Fusiliers Museum, Bury: Major A. J. Maher MBE at the Queen's Lancashire Regiment Museum at Preston: Lieutenant Colonel T. C. E. Vines, The Prince of Wales's Own Regiment of Yorkshire at York.

In the chapter on Spion Kop quotations are made from Corporal Walter Herbert's letter, which is from the collection of The King's Own Royal Regiment Museum, Lancaster; and from the Lancashire Fusiliers collection, the piece entitled simply, 'Spion Kop', written by the then Lieutenant Colonel C. J. Blomfield DSO.

Among more general museums and libraries: Dr. J. Vincent of Province of Kwazulu-Natal Department of Education and Culture Museum Service, Pietermaritzburg, South Africa; The National Army Museum, Chelsea including Dr. P. B. Boyden, Joan Bennet, and the other marvellously helpful ladies in the Reading Room. I thank the Director of the War Museum of the Boer Republics, Col Jacobs, and his Deputy Mr. J. H. du Pisani for permission to use the unique tiles as a front cover. Mr Dave Erasmus of *The Natal Witness,* South Africa's oldest newspaper, was very helpful, as were the SATOUR Tour Guides, Mrs Spiret and Messrs. Sneyman and Watts of that organisation. In turn, they led me to Doug McMasters, who, in turn led me to Harts Hill, giving me his time and a view of his splendid Blockhouse Museum in the process.

My wife has shown great long suffering which must be

acknowledged; D. P. Everitt of Redcar is to be thanked for his proof-reading and welcome criticism, and last but not least, Roni Wilkinson of Pen and Sword for his slave-driving and criticizing, also very welcome!

Advice for Tourers

Distance, it is said, lends enchantment, and that is especially true of South Africa, for it is far away in distance and in time. Whilst I was writing this early in 1997 the manager of a team of sportsmen returning from that land was heard to remark that when in South Africa you are cocooned from what is happening elsewhere. When corresponding with persons in that land the writer has had to cultivate patience and expect weeks to elapse before a response is obtained.

So, to visit is a great adventure and part of that adventure is that we are among the earliest of a new breed of visitors, at a time when things are settling down to what looks like a new and more promising order. The fact remains, though, that the first thing that needs to be mentioned is security.

The visitor finds that South Africans in general want visitors to be happy in their land and are very helpful. They have a great interest in being hospitable, so take advantage of their invaluable 'on the ground' comments upon the places which you intend to visit. Safety in some areas cannot be taken for granted, so it is sound preparation, upon arrival, to talk to the local people about security in the areas on the itinerary. Of course, it may be that they have a vested interest in persuading you that visitors are safe, or on the other hand you may be unfortunate enough to receive a diatribe about the state of their country and you will be none the wiser as to the truth; but you should listen to them and then apply normal common sense.

The options for travel to that land are improving all the time with the resultant benefits brought by competition. Probably, Battlefield visitors will enter via Johannesburg or Durban and these and Ladysmith are the only big cities likely to be visited. Ladysmith has some of the atmosphere of a large country town but even here it could be possible to be in the wrong place, as it were. There are areas where there is more likelihood of being threatened, but as a tourist one should expect to avoid them and also to obey the conventional wisdom of not throwing money about in public places, nor flaunting expensive equipment and so forth. An enticing entertainment or eating place should be considered carefully, but sound thinking will help the visitor to avoid danger.

Majuba Hill where the British suffered a humiliating reverse at the hands of the burghers on 27th February 1881. It became the taunt and battle-cry for both sides during the Boer War.

Johannesburg and Durban newspapers regularly carry reports of muggings but would you and your friends feel safe in all districts in your own city, and does the English press not carry daily stories of violent assault?

The reason for travelling being to visit the battlefields, we should consider if these are safe in themselves. They are all in country places. When my wife and I visited Chieveley and Clouston there were very few people about, similarly at Spearman's, but these places felt safe – whatever that implies. Spion Kop is as lonely as Kinderscout in Derbyshire and yet we felt safe there, too, in fact more so. The Tugela Heights, which is important to the story, is a jumble of hills and we were told that this remote section can be dangerous.

If there are any doubts about a given area, consider hiring a guide. Ask at the local Tourism Bureau, or at the Ladysmith Siege Museum, for the phone number of an official South African Tour Guide, or look for their advertisement on the hotel notice board. In 1996 we understood that they charged typically R35 per hour to join a car group, or there are coach parties. We met a guide at Clouston, a gentleman of Boer background, and found him to be well informed and even-handed in his story-telling. He was also very kind to us and welcomed us to listen to his recounting of the Battle of Colenso. When he learned that I had a problem with the exact location of Colonel Long's guns he was very willing to lead us there, with the approval of the gentleman who was employing him that morning. A visitor can rely on them to know their business.

You will need a car and the writer has found it best to use an international company and book in the UK by credit card, using a local travel agent. The more commercial allies you have the better.

Those used to renting cars in the USA will note the differences here: the Americans may not know what another currency other than the dollar is, but they will accept travellers cheques as money. The credit card is king and distances and liquids are familiarly measured in miles and gallons. In South Africa travellers cheques are changed at banks and cannot be used as cash, and credit cards can not be used to buy

General Colley with a small body of troops, including the Gordon Highlanders, scaled Majuba Hill, which dominated the Boer laager. When dawn broke the British shouted insults at the sleepy burghers who recovered quickly from their shock, counter attacked and drove the British off with withering rifle fire. Below an artist's impression of the action depicts the rout.

petrol, so these are factors in deciding how much ready cash to carry. Mind you, after European prices, the price of fuel will be a relief and will go some way to offsetting the expensive cost of car-hire. Driving in South Africa has similar pros and cons to those it has in the USA, in that the urban expressways are crowded and confusing to the stranger, with the rest of the roads often quite empty, but the South African custom of driving on the left is an added bonus to the UK traveller.

The collection and deposit of rental cars is very easy, as in North America, though how difficult it is when returning a damaged car is not personally known, thank goodness! Do not be afraid to show ignorance to the bright young people who are at the desk; ask them questions as they are patient and very glad to help. Before leaving the hirer's office make sure that the procedure to adopt in the case of breakdown is clear and that the public telephone system is understood.

But still, as travellers, the question of security has not gone away, so:

Do fill up as often as possible, at well-frequented garages.

Do not give lifts.

Avoid driving at night because there are long lonely stretches to cover and also because of the disconcerting way in which Africans walk for miles and can be found walking along, well into the road, at all hours and in dark clothes.

At all times be prepared for animals on the road such as cattle, which can be found grazing on the verges.

Beware of long vehicles which seem less well-marked than in Britain, and note that there are more dilapidated cars about generally.

The South African unit of currency is the Rand and is indicated by 'R' before the value, where we write £ when meaning sterling. All values shown in this book are based on the exchange rate of Autumn 1996, R6.9 = £1 so fluctuations should be allowed for. In October 1997, for instance, the value was R7.34 = £1, and in March 1998 R8.0.

The preparation will have included contact with the South African Tourist people (SATOUR) and we found that they will supply a basic planning map, but the local Tourist Associations may well have more useful maps once in the area. The Thukela Joint Services Board, PO Box 116, Ladysmith 3370 has a very serviceable one covering Thukela (the modern name for what the white-dominated past called "Tugela"). This they will send you, or to buy it locally is very cheap. Then the Publicity Associations on "The Battlefields Route" have extensive selections of guides and maps. However, they are not detailed and in places like Tugela Heights the ground view can be very confusing –

Ladysmith, the goal of the Natal Field Force. This view, from Convent Hill, shows the clock tower of the Town Hall, peeping up at bottom left, and now long restored from the Boer shelling. Privates Scott and Pitts, the Manchester VCs, would recognize it – but they would not find the cricket field for that is under the large white building to the left. They would know the pavilion, which is preserved, but in this view hidden by the trees. They would definately recognize Caesar's Camp, the hill in the background, where they won their decorations and helped save the day in the attack of 6th January 1900.

which is another reason to consult the Satour Guides.

The distance from Durban to Ladysmith is 235 kilometres via the N3 and N11 and, if there is time available, there are accessible en route other places where good museums are to be found, as well as places important to the build-up of the story such as Pietermaritzburg. Indeed, if you were tempted to 'fork right' in Durban, 120 kilometres later and twenty years earlier we would be in a completely different and equally exciting campaign – the Zulu War of 1879!

Buller here reading despatches, could equally well have been planning tonight's billet.

Johannesburg to Ladysmith is 391 kilometres and if at the planning stage it is decided that a view of Majuba Hill is essential to the flavour of the visit one could take the Highway 23 aiming for the N11. This does not look as direct as the N3 but runs down towards the south-eastern corner of Transvaal and Volksrust. You might have in mind towns like Heidelberg, Balfour, Standerton and Volksrust itself as possible places to try for lodgings when you have had enough driving, and could judge where to stop for the night.

The British visitor will plan based on the time of arrival as well as the place. The writer has flown in to Johannesburg at midday and has known that the airport could be left and the appropriate road found quickly with a reasonable target town in mind. Any doubts whatsoever about the capability of doing this, or any arrival into the country at later times, demand a plan for a short journey on a clear route to a pre-booked hotel.

It will be found that hotel prices (although the sky is the limit, of course) can be much more easily afforded that in the UK though, come to that, it seems that this is true of most of the world! Enquiry at the British headquarters of international chains and the South African Tourist Department/ local tourist offices produces helpful assistance. The tourist and information people in places like Ladysmith, Dundee, Colenso, or for that matter Ulundi (for the 1879 Zulu battlefields), are homely, courteous and genuinely helpful. For visitors they will produce a mountain of pamphlets and handouts and they will not be stingy. Among the advice given will be the clear injunction to avoid downtown Johannesburg if at all possible. We made sure it was possible. Similar injunctions would be made about parts of Durban, without doubt.

Out of season, which is basically March to September, lodgings are usually easily available and the writer has found this to be true in South Africa as in many other lands, provided the search starts early enough. One or two calls at, say, four o'clock or so, will find a reasonably priced room. There are the top class hotels, of course, advertised in the Tourist Board's handouts, but also comfortable pensions are available, chalet sites and even purpose-built Zulu kraals in some places, clean but very basic, with shared toilet and kitchen blocks. B&Bs abound. They are, by British standards well-priced, and the ones that we have used combined that quality with conditions that range from very nice to palatial. Especially to be treasured is the fact that the home, possibly a bungalow, often stands in a very large garden with opportunity for a civilized al fresco cuppa in the morning or evening, although this is qualified by the remarks later about the climate.

Typical prices for one night were as follows. A hotel with an internationally known name, though not at the top of the range, inclusive of dinner, bed and help-yourself breakfast, charged £51.84 for two people in 1996. In a small country hotel, an en suite room with an excellent four course dinner, and breakfast consisting of the full works including fresh fruit, was £36.51 for two people. Beautiful picnic lunches were offered too. A B&B offering similar breakfasts as well as a glass of wine and evening socializing in the fine kitchen was in the region of £23 for two without dinner. The room was comfortable with good quality furnishings and kettle, tea and coffee. Again it was

Replica Creusot 150mm gun outside Ladysmith Town Hall and the Siege Museum. Behind is an elderly British Howitzer pressed into service as a response.

en suite with its own front door as well as the entrance through the house; but with the curious feature of not having a door between its bathroom and the bedroom: not even a door frame... The furnishings and hospitality were fine and directions to eating places, advice on safety and the shortest time to a certain site were readily forthcoming. The motels were of varying standards as you would expect, but the food, down to bar-meals, was very good, well done and generous.

It is stressed that this was out of season, in late September and mid March, and in season an increase of possibly 25% could be expected.

Entering Kwazulu-Natal from the Volkrust direction brings the visitor straight into the Natal theatre of the war and Newcastle, Laings Nek, Allemans Nek, Dundee and then the battlefields associated with the relief of Ladysmith are at very short distances. Further away to the east, but easily done from Dundee by different roads, are Rorke's Drift and the dramatic Isandlwana. Ulundi, and the rest of the sites associated with the Zulu War of 1879, require a different base, but the principles discussed here apply to that area though hotel selection needs a little more care.

The weather is very strange by British standards and it should be remembered that this part of Natal is tucked under the Drakensberg Mountain range. The winters are dry and can be cold with snow on higher ground and severe frosts at night, whereas the summers are very hot, though even then it can be cold at night. The other feature of the summer climate is the generation of spectacular rainstorms which occur quite regularly. In accounts of the Boer War the men are constantly suffering badly from the sun and are short of water, or are soaking wet and cold, suffering the further discomfort of having to allow their clothes to dry on their backs. Happily you should be able to avoid that.

However, obviously there is a need for warm but removable clothing for the winter, and light summer wear with a woollen jumper for the evenings or to put on when the rain brings the temperature down. Naturally you must have a good raincoat and more than one pair of sound footwear.

The jabs recommended by your GP will have been endured well enough in advance, and malaria tablets taken, and you will have a quality insect-repellent. A first aid kit, camera, compass, note-books and pens, pencils etc. are 'musts', a torch is useful and, if possible, binoculars. Adequate travel insurance is a must.

The appropriate advice seems to be that alertness and caution is required at all times, but one should give the people and the country an opportunity to be as kind as they really are.

Useful addresses have included,

Colenso Information Office,
PO Box 213,
Colenso 3360

Dundee Publicity Association,
Private Bag X2024,
Dundee 3000,

Ladysmith Publicity Association,
PO Box 1307,
Ladysmith 3370,

Ladysmith Siege Museum,
PO Box 29,
Ladysmith 3370

Ulundi Tourism and Publicity,
PO Box 261,
Ulundi 3838,
Kwazulu-Natal,
South Africa.

Chapter One

THE BACKGROUND

The Boer War of 1899/1902 was precipitated for the same reasons as the others, with the added spice provided by the receipt of an unexpected inheritance.

On the Afrikander side the reason was the wish not to have to submit to British rule, restrictive as they found it to be, and a desire to keep the native inhabitants in their territories in subjection: a domination akin to slavery. As to the first feeling, they still saw the British as foreigners, even after a relationship going back 100 years or so – their language was different, their way of life was different and their laws were different. Previous incomers had been people like themselves: escapees from Europe's pressure, persecuted ones looking for their own place, or just those longing for the chance to be free, all of these could be assimilated. The Huguenots, those persecuted French protestants, were the main case in point.

The British, on the other hand, came as an occupying power when Holland fell into the hands of Napoleon, and the Boers feared that they themselves would be assimilated.

One aspect of British law covered the ownership of slaves, and in 1834 the abolition of slavery in British colonies meant that the Boers' view of the natives became intolerable, so the original white inhabitants began the Great Trek from 1835 onwards. Around 5,000 Boer men, women and children and as many 'servants' crossed the Orange and then the Vaal River to find a new land free of London and Cape meddling. They were followed by thousands more.

To be fair, many of their brothers and sisters stayed where they were, no doubt because they had made a go of it, in spite of the British; had built up farms and other businesses which were too good to leave. They paid their taxes and 'worked the system,' but even they were always a concern to the government and had to be reckoned with.

The wanderers, God's People, for that is how they saw themselves, looked for their own milk and honey, undergoing indescribable hardships as they did so.

The weather in South Africa is often very hot with strong sunshine, but, as noted in the last chapter, in summertime there are also torrential downpours, which may be bitter cold, and the winter nights are even colder. All this they were used to, and it could be endured in a mean

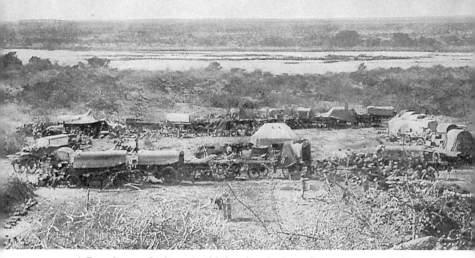

A Boer laager during a 'trek' showing the long Cape wagons pulled into a defensive box. Cattle are tethered in the centre and thorn bushes have been cut and placed in the gaps between the wheels.

hovel among a familiar jumble of rocks. A fire and a dry place to sleep can make the hardest living tolerable, and mostly they ate heavily with plenty of meat and corn-based fare. Once on trek, though, it was very different, for they lived any way they could, providing the way was forward, solely by the gun, and they had to adapt all the time. It was no hardship to feed on and enjoy uncooked, sun-dried meat called biltong – indeed, enjoy it they still do – and if need be they could eat the food of the earlier inhabitants. But victuals could be short and insufficient to fuel their sturdy frames. The sun beat down upon them or the rain soaked them until the sun dried them off again as their bullocks dragged the huge wagons over roadless veldt and scarp alike. These cumbersome vehicles had to be floated across great rivers where, even to get to the water, they had to be hauled down vertically into the ravine's bottom and pulled up the further side again with much use of whip and slave. At night the wagons were heaved into a great circle, or laager, and sentries were set while men, women and little ones slept.

It is interesting that this pioneer activity by white men in South Africa coincides with similar tales of hard times and amazing displays of fortitude and determination in North America. There the dispossessed, the poor and the adventurous, augmented by a body unknown to the South African Voortrekkers, namely, new foreigners – British, German, Scandinavian and others who had just arrived on the continent – were making their way over the Great Plains and southern

Wyoming, only to face the Rocky Mountains on the way to their Promised Land, Oregon.

A problem faced both groups: somebody else was already using the land. Maybe they were using it in a different way, but it was in use. The native American's use was quite unlike that of the white people, but the intention of the native African was very similar to that of the Boers; cattle breeding. New American and Boer alike recognized their huge problem – but found it to be no more daunting than the lack of map or road, the unforgiving weather, the diseases from unknown causes obvious to us, and all the other hardships on the way. At least they had faith in God – and firearms.

The Boers found a good land which would respond to work (and none could question their dedication to work); a beautiful land with variety of form. When they got to the high hills near the Tugela River they climbed a flat top and saw, like Moses in Nebo, a land made for their habitation. The Portuguese had called the country Natal when they first saw it from the sea to the east; the Boers named the viewpoint Lookout Hill: Spion Kop.

Leaving behind scattered families who had decided that this was their place, the body pressed on with British interests following them, the fierce Zulus in front of them. Initially defeated by the latter, marksmanship overcame the current landowners at Blood River on 16th December 1838 and the Boers were the new masters – except that the interfering Anglos came on again and in 1842 took control of the area known as Natal along with its potentially important harbour at Durban.

Numbers of Dutch, now settled on lonely farms, stayed put, but the trek re-commenced and, after crossing the Vaal, the body of the travellers founded several small republics with quaint names and primitive organizations before there appeared the Republics of Transvaal and Orange Free State.

Again Britain had an interest and, though she recognized the two governments in 1852 and 1854 respectively, she kept a careful eye on their doings. As they, especially Transvaal, fell deeper and deeper into financial problems, partly because of the Boers' propensity to chafe even at their own government, London annexed the Transvaal, with some opposition.

A kind of status quo obtained for some years until, partly for the benefit of the Dutch farmers in Natal, London decided to break the Zulu military system once and for all and destroy the house of Shaka. King Cetshwayo, against his better judgement, was manoeuvred into a

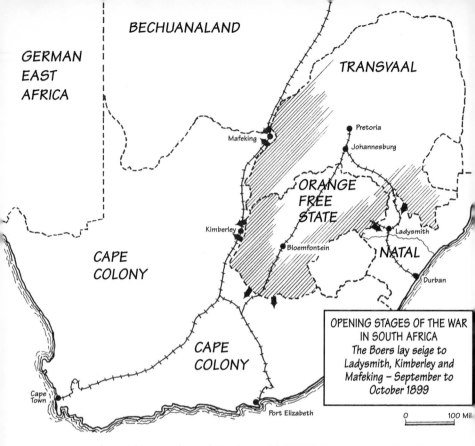

BECHUANALAND

GERMAN
EAST
AFRICA

TRANSVAAL

Pretoria
Mafeking
Johannesburg

ORANGE
FREE
STATE

Kimberley
Ladysmith
Bloemfontein
NATAL

CAPE
COLONY
Durban

OPENING STAGES OF THE WAR
IN SOUTH AFRICA
The Boers lay seige to
Ladysmith, Kimberley and
Mafeking – September to
October 1899

CAPE
COLONY

Cape
Town

Port Elizabeth
0   100 Mil

war he could not win and by the end of 1879 there was no threat to
Britain in the colony of Natal.

The Boers however, far from being grateful, now saw their chance
to throw off British controls. A weak British government and
generalship was exposed by underestimated farmers who also
happened to be well-mounted and armed, in a war that lasted from
December 1880 to February 1881.

In August of that year the Liberal Government of Mr. Gladstone
conceded independence on what many saw as terms ignominious to
the British. The Boers appeared to have freed themselves once and for
all.

And it was now that the unexpected inheritance appeared.

* * * * *

The British reason for the Boer War of 1899 was quite different.
They came to South Africa, not as the defeated and unenfranchised,

but as enemies and stayed as victors, for the Cape was theirs as a spoil of Napoleon's war. It was a valuable prize for Britain to secure; her trade with India and the Orient called for a watering-place on the way and a base for the navy in its world-wide role, and this spot was ideal. Further, they paid for the place in a legitimate British fashion, £6,000,000 to be exact.

By 1820 British settlers were arriving and for some fifty years the English and Dutch speaking peoples doggedly improved their situation. The black man, if not a slave after Abolition, still provided the next grade of labour required above the animal level, and was very much a second class citizen. Had the Boers seen him as a man at all he would have been a third class citizen as they, Boers, were often depicted by the British as dirty and idle, while we have seen what the Boers thought of the British.

In 1867 a new influence was revealed with the discovery of diamonds at Hopetown, Cape Colony, and the rush continued with another find in Griqualand West in 1870 leading the British to annex the area the year after. In 1877, when Transvaal was almost bankrupted by native wars, the British annexed it.

As already noted, after the Zulu War the Boers felt strong enough to strike at British occupation and on 20th December 1880 British troops were ambushed or besieged. The unthinkable happened, and a world power was humiliated at Majuba Hill on 27th February 1881.

At home the public was outraged, but the Government was defeated at the hustings and the incoming Liberal Party gave back to Transvaal her independence on the condition that the British controlled its foreign policy. In the great world diplomatic struggle which was heavily concerned with Africa, it was a day for Britain's European competitors to cheer.

In 1884 the Convention of London re-defined certain points and the main ones for our purpose were that any Boer guarantees on natives' rights disappeared on the one hand, and on the other the Transvaal's westward growth was limited by the British being allowed to control the territory next door, the arid Bechuanaland. This was a very important step for the British as further west again was new German territory secured by Bismarck and beside the Atlantic Ocean. By relinquishing any pretence to a watchful eye over the Boers' treatment of the natives, the prevention of a junction between an opponent, Transvaal, and a possible enemy, Germany, was thwarted.

Gradually the flame was being turned up on the European power-struggle in Africa, and Britain, in spite of great reservations in high places, had to keep an eye on her competitors' activities further north. The Boer Republics, being wayward, and poverty-stricken, were always a potential danger in their possible friendly relations with these competitors. The annexing of Bechuanaland, west of Transvaal, stopped that with the northern part becoming a British protectorate and the southern a Crown Colony.

One of the most powerful men in South Africa at this time was Cecil John Rhodes. In 1884 he was 31; miner, entrepreneur, businessman, tycoon, politician and a whole lot more besides. In 1883 he had described Bechuanaland to the Cape Parliament as the key to the Colony becoming the most powerful state in southern Africa. Privately, he saw it as essential to the fulfilment of his dream of having the whole of Africa under British control.

* * * * *

Now, at this fluid stage, there was revealed the inheritance noted at the start. The Boers found that they were sitting on a gold-mine, literally, as in September 1886 the Transvaal Gold Rush began. The Boers and the British had reason enough to be in opposite camps, but now these unexpected developments brought together the Boer and British reasons for coming to war.

And Rhodes was in on the ground floor.

He and the Boers knew one another and they, with everyone else, watched his progress – a part of the steps to war. In 1888, by dubious means, he secured mining concessions from King Lobengula in the territories north of Bechuanaland, stoking his dream of British control continuously from the Cape northwards across east-central Africa, through the Sudan to Egypt and the Mediterranean Sea. The two Boer Republics were now both surrounded by what was, to all intents and purposes, British property. In that same year he and Beit, the 'Gold Bug', joined their interests in Kimberley and formed De Beers Consolidated.

Cecil John Rhodes
1853-1902

1890 was a big year for Cecil Rhodes. He was Prime Minister of the Cape, and his men moved into Mashonaland and founded Salisbury. That Lobengula had been cheated mattered not a jot. By 1893 the actual reason for war was in place for the world to see. All this imperialism surrounded the burgeoning gold-mining business. The Transvaal was no longer bankrupt and the new President, Paul Kruger, veteran of Blood River and victor of the war of 1881 was in place for the third term.

Taxes were paid... but still not by the veldt farmers, and not eagerly by the burghers. Now though there was a small army of tax-payers on hand – Uitlanders, or foreigners. The gold had brought this change as well. They were needed to operate the mines, they and the army of black labour, still nearly slaves but earning the minimum that could be got away with. The Uitlanders could argue that they were the real wealth creators by their labour, but were then required to make the strongest support to the state's coffers. Yet in that state they had no voice.

The individualism and righteous self-confidence that had brought the Boers all this way easily saw the red lights shining when the foreign engineers and senior mine staff wanted the vote. They would end up with control of the country.

Stephanus Johannes Paulus Kruger
1825-1904

The Boers had, as always, their intransigence to fall back on. The Uitlanders had Rhodes and his people, led by his malleable doctor and close associate, Leander Starr Jameson.

A plan was hatched for an Uitlander rising in order to secure their demands – to coincide with an invasion by Dr. Jameson and a band of Rhodesian Police launched from Bechuanaland. In the shadows at the back of the plan was Rhodes, and further back in a recess was none other than Joseph Chamberlain, Colonial Secretary in Lord Salisbury's administration. Of course, Rhodes did not want to be visible until the prizes were given out, and Chamberlain just did not want to be visible but would find a good result very satisfactory. He did not get one.

The Uitlanders did not rise and Uncle Paul got wind of the 'Jameson Raid,' for that is what it was, and the Rhodesian Police had to surrender to the Transvaalers.

Rhodes was palpably implicated, though he shielded Chamberlain, and Kruger's hand strengthened when he handed over the raiders to the Crown to be dealt with. They were jailed and Rhodes had to resign as Prime Minister of Cape Colony.

Kruger was now involved in distant discussion with the Colonial Secretary and found himself up against a man as cunning and single-minded as himself, Sir Alfred Milner, the British High Commissioner. So dissembling was Milner, indeed, that his boss was thwarted and so was *his* boss, Lord Salisbury, the Prime Minister. In the moments when Uncle Paul thought the game was up and appeared ready to concede the Uitlanders the vote, Milner put obstacles in the way so that his objective, war with the Boers, could be attained. Thus, he thought, could the Empire's interests be served.

Kruger meanwhile and his Commandant-General, Joubert, with the

Sir Alfred Milner, the British High Commissioner, and his staff.

Orange Free State Artillery at the start of the war.

proceeds from the mines, were now in a position to import arms; the best. The latest Mauser rifles were introduced in large quantities using false documents and falsely labelled cases, along with the newest smokeless ammunition. The newest artillery was also introduced, manned by professional gunners. Included were Krupp's and Creusot's 75mm guns which could fire a 14.$\frac{1}{2}$lb high explosive shell for nearly five miles, Creusot's 115mm guns which cast an 88 lb high explosive shell some 6.$\frac{1}{4}$ miles and Creusot 150mm fortress guns firing 94 lb shells. Added to these were the pompoms bought under the nose of the British Government.

For the sake of comparison we could here note that the British employed the Naval guns from the cruiser *Terrible*, namely 4.7″ with their 45lb shells which could be charged with high explosive or shrapnel and had a range of over 5$\frac{1}{2}$ miles, and 12 pounders sending **Maxim or 'pompom' gun. This effective weapon was bought under the nose of the British Government.**

HMS *Powerful*, sister ship of HMS *Terrible* whose guns were used by the Naval Brigade.

Naval Brigade and a 4.7″ gun – straw hats, naval-made wheels and all – cross a drift.

high explosive shells some 4½ miles. Then there were the Army's own 12 pounders firing 12½ lb shells two miles; 15 pounders firing 14lb shrapnel shells up to over two miles, and 5″ Howitzers which sent a 50 lb shell two and three quarter miles.

So now the Boers had ample reason to feel themselves about to be assimilated into an Empire that they did not want to join but felt confident that they had certain strong cards to play. The British, for their part, had a position to keep up, within the sight of the other European Empires. Oh, and then there was the welfare of the natives to consider. At least, it was said there was in 1899, though by 1902, at the Peace settlement at Vereeniging, that seems to have been forgotten.

It was time to stop talking and to start riding.

On Thursday 12th October Joubert's men began to move south west over the passes into Natal. On the 20th the British allowed them to attack at Talana Hill, Dundee and though the British beat them off, it

Three Boer Generals: De Wet, De La Rey and Botha.

seemed right to the British command to withdraw the troops further south to Ladysmith. By November the Boers had laid siege to Kimberley, Mafeking and Ladysmith as well.

From today's perspective these look like errors, and in Natal, Durban should have been the real objective but instead the Siege of Ladysmith became, for both sides, an object in itself: for one, the glory of the capitulation of numbers of British regulars with their stores; for the other the end to an impertinent affront. The British in particular had some learning to do and it was a pity that they did not pay more attention to the man they had chosen to sort the mess out – General Sir Redvers Buller. They had to learn what he clearly knew: whatever they were the Boers were not impertinent; rather, well-prepared and equipped, diligent and intelligent.

The lessons started on 'Mournful Monday', 30th October, and three other sessions were due in 'Black Week', commencing Sunday 10th December. One was at Stormberg in the Cape Colony, the second at Magersfontein on the Cape Colony/Orange Free State border, and we are particularly interested in the third.

> *But it's 'Special train for Atkins' when the trooper's*
> *on the tide –*
> *The troopship's on the tide, my boys, the troopship's*
> *on the tide.*
> *O it's special train for Atkins when the troopship's*
> *on the tide.*
>
> Rudyard Kipling

The Rifle Brigade sail from Southampton for South Africa in SS *German*.

Chapter Two

COLENSO
15th December 1900

Buller landed in Cape Town on 31st October and quickly decided that his command should be split into three. Lieutenant-General Lord Methuen took the 1st Division north-west to the Orange River on the way to relieve Kimberley. Lieutenant-General Sir C. F. Clery and the 2nd Division was in Natal and Major-General Sir William Gatacre commanded the 3rd Division in Cape Colony where there were enemy

Lieutenant-General Lord Methuen 1ST DIVISION	Lieutenant-General Sir C F Clery 2ND DIVISION	Major-General Sir W F Gatacre, KCB 3RD DIVISION

troops present and where the 'loyal' Boers were a worry too. On 22nd November 1899 Sir Redvers Buller left the Cape himself and went to Natal where the Boers were building strong fortifications along the Tugela River. He knew from previous service here that the Boers were highly capable and he recognized that, though he had a large army, the enemy were well equipped and in a very strong position. He still did not know how well-placed and how well led they were, for a genius had appeared among them in the shape of Louis Botha, who was to feature prominently right to the end of the war. When it ended, he would help direct the nation's affairs under the British crown to the end of his life.

On 13th December General Buller's Intelligence Staff estimated that about 6000 to 7000 men had been concentrated under Louis Botha in the neighbourhood.

From Potgieter's Drift in the west to 30 miles east of Colenso a range of high, broken ground makes a continuous wall. It is pierced by gullies and at its eastern end by three roads from Colenso to Ladysmith through difficult country. Louis Botha, delegated by Generals Erasmus and Prinsloo, had prepared over a period of three weeks a trench system on a line north of the Tugela, and roughly extending east across and south of it to a large hill called Mount Hlangwane. Using armies

After encircling Ladysmith the Boers, under General Botha, established a line of defence along the Tugela River and awaited the British attempts to raise the siege.

DRAKENBERG MOUNTAINS

TELE

DEWDROP

KRANTZ KLOOF

ON

BN
HOMES

THREE TREE HILL

SPION KOP

BRAKFONTEIN

VAAL KRANTZ

WAGON DRIFT
TRICHARDS DRIFT

SPEARMAN'S HILL

POTGEITERS DRIFT

SWARTZ KOP

MOUNT ALICE

SPEARMAN'S FARM

MARITZ FERRY

Louis Botha

TUG

of Africans forced into service, it was dug near to the river bank with dummy trenches on the crests of the backing hills, where the British would expect the defending force to be. For the most part the works were invisible, apart from the terraces of trenches at the foot of Fort Wylie at the north end of the railway bridge. During each night the guns were moved about from one position to another. The Boers felt that they were completely hidden, even as far as protection from

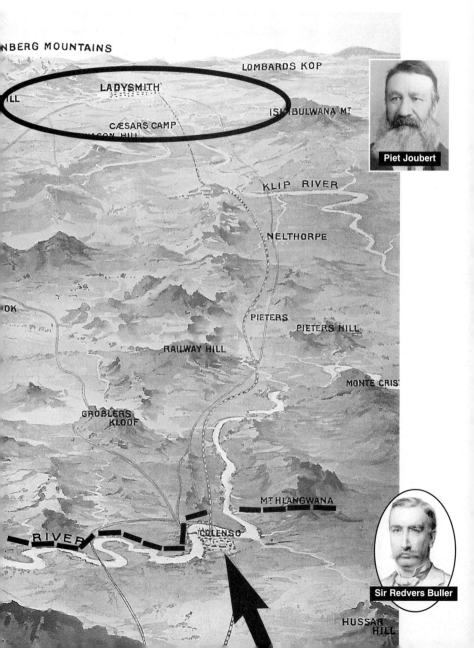

artillery using the new Lyddite high explosive or shrapnel. To get maximum value from these preparations Botha repeated the instructions given him by the supreme commander, Piet Joubert: 'on the day of battle do not shoot too early'. No shots of any kind were to be fired until Botha caused the great howitzer to be fired. The line was manned by, from west to east, the men from the Orange Free State, the Johannesburg and the Middleburg Commando; then the Zoutpansberg Commando opposite the Bridle Drift; the Swaziland and Ermelo Commandos at Punt Drift with more Middleburgers; the Boksburgers by Bulwer Bridge; the Heidelberg, Vryheid and Krugersdorp Commandos north of the village of Colenso, and the Wakkerstroom and Standerton Commandos on Hlangwane.

From Ladysmith to Colenso is about 30 kilometres by today's road R103 and that was to prove to be a long way for Sir Redvers Buller. The writer has approached the town of Colenso from Winterton (in Buller's time called Springfield) which is about 35 kilometres along the R74, crossing over the N3 Toll Road, and then to the Estcourt turnoff. Here is where Botha derailed a train and captured Winston Churchill and, if one was to turn right, Frere village would be quickly reached. The advantage in coming up from Pietermaritzburg or, if travelling south from Ladysmith, of detouring via Winterton, is that you see the Tugela Line as Buller first saw it. Approaching from Winterton be aware of the higher ground away to the right, but it is well back and you are in rolling open country with little enough cover; entirely unlike the broken ground seen to the left beyond the Tugela.

The line from Pietermaritzberg and Durban comes from the right on this photo and sweeps round to the right to run beside the R74 road from Springfield (now Winterton) towards Colenso.

THIS MARKS THE PLACE WHERE THE ARMOURED TRAIN WAS WRECKED AND THE RT. HON. WINSTON CHURCHILL CAPTURED BY BOER FORCES NOV. 15TH 1899.

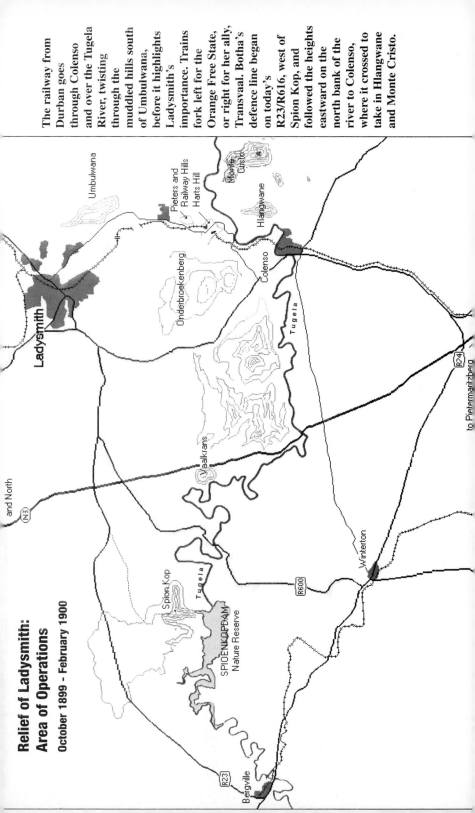

Relief of Ladysmith: Area of Operations

October 1899 - February 1900

The railway from Durban goes through Colenso and over the Tugela River, twisting through the muddled hills south of Umbulwana, before it highlights Ladysmith's importance. Trains fork left for the Orange Free State, or right for her ally, Transvaal. Botha's defence line began on today's R23/R616, west of Spion Kop, and followed the heights eastward on the north bank of the river to Colenso, where it crossed to take in Hlangwane and Monte Cristo.

Umbulwana

Ladysmith

Onderbroekenberg

Peters and Railway Hills
Harts Hill

Monte Cristo

Hlangwane

Colenso

Tugela

and North

N3

Vaalkrans

Tugela

Spion Kop

Tugela

SPIOENKOPDAM
Nature Reserve

Winterton

R600

R23

Bergville

R24

to Pietermaritzberg

Earl of Dundonald

**Major-General
Hildyard**

**Lieut-General
Hon N G Lyttelton**

**Major-General
Fitzroy Hart**

**Major-General
G Barton**

At Frere, Natal, Buller had at his disposal the following:

Mounted Brigade of some 1800 men, under Colonel Douglas Mackinnon Bailie Hamilton Cochrane, the twelfth Earl of Dundonald. These comprised:
> Royal Dragoons.
> 13th Hussars.
> Thorneycroft's Regiment of Mounted Infantry.
> Bethune's Regiment of Mounted Infantry.
> Naval Brigade under Captain E. P. Jones RN, (HMS Forte), with attached Natal Volunteers.
>> **2** x 4.7″ guns and **14** x 12 pdr 12 cwt guns

Field Artillery
1st Brigade Div., 7th, 14th and 66th Batteries under Lieutenant Colonel H. V. Hunt.
2nd Brigade Div., 64th and 73rd Batteries under Lieutenant Colonel L. W. Parsons.

Infantry
2nd Brigade under Major-General H.J.T. Hildyard, composed of
> 2nd Battalion Royal West Surrey Regiment
> 2nd Battalion Devonshire Regiment
> 2nd Battalion West Yorkshire Regiment.
> 2nd Battalion East Surrey Regiment.

4th Brigade under Major-General the Hon N. G. Lyttelton, composed of
> 2nd Battalion Scottish Rifles.
> 3rd Battalion Kings Royal Rifle Corps
> 1st Battalion Durham Light Infantry
> 1st Battalion Rifle Brigade

5th Brigade under Major-General A. Fitzroy Hart, composed of
> 1st Battalion Royal Inniskilling Fusiliers
> 1st Battalion The Border Regiment
> 1st Battalion The Connaught Rangers
> 2nd Battalion Royal Dublin Fusiliers

6th Brigade under Major-General G. Barton, composed of
> 2nd Battalion Royal Fusiliers
> 2nd Battalion Royal Scots Fusiliers
> 1st Battalion Royal Welsh Fusiliers
> 2nd Battalion Royal Irish Fusiliers

Also 17th coy. Royal Engineers; and "A" Pontoon Troop

According to the *History of the War in South Africa* by Major-General Sir Fredrick Maurice KCB published in 1906, Buller had an army of 19,378 officers and men under his command with 5555 horses.

So, here, Buller collected his force, at the sleepy railway halt of Frere. A village which had already been startled by the Boers having blown the bridge and looted the houses, now had the bucolic quiet

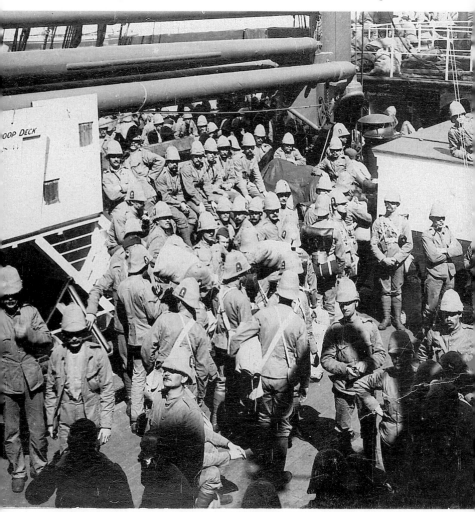

British troops on board ship en-route for Durban. They were soon to find that their opponents, the Boer farmers, were more than a match for them in tactics and marksmanship.

completely shattered by an armed host. Buller may have had a large army, but he had a large problem too. He could not avoid the natural river barrier that had now become the Tugela Line and he had to find the easiest and cheapest approach. Sir George White, GOC Natal, telegraphed him from Ladysmith to suggest that he took the most westerly route through by the valley of the Onderbroek Spruit. Buller favoured an approach much further west via Potgieter's Drift, but felt that the news of the recent defeats at Magersfontein and at Stormberg in the Cape Colony made this plan dangerous. It would involve a march of over forty miles with his long tail of ox wagons menaced by a watching enemy full of confidence, so he rejected it in favour of the route suggested by White. By the afternoon of 14th December, the

'Footsloggin over Africa' (Kipling). Here an infantry company, intent on relieving Ladysmith, heads for the Boer blocking line positioned on the Tugela River.

army was on the plain in front of the tin-roofed village of Colenso, opposite the curve of the Tugela River between that town and Bridle Drift.

*If approaching from Winterton you will have driven a part of that difficult forty miles as far as Frere and now are in the area that the great army occupied. Beyond the junction with the Estcourt road (R103) pass the sign that points to the Battle of Blaukrantz between the Zulus and the Voortrekkers in 1838, and then, with the railway on the right, come to the sign that says, **Chieveley Station**, and **Chieveley Military Cemetery**. It is important not to miss this as its location helps to get the size of the operation and to imagine the immensity of the area it occupied. It is also the resting place of Lord Roberts' son. **Turn right** at the sign over the railway tracks, and **right again** on a rutted farm track across the plain. There are dilapidated properties beside*

ANGLO-BOER WAR 1899-1902
MILITARY HOSPITAL, CHIEVELEY

IN THIS VICINITY, AT NO. 4 STATIONARY MILITARY HOSPITAL, ALL THE BRITISH WOUNDED IN THE BATTLES OF COLENSO (15 DECEMBER 1899) AND TUGELA HEIGHTS (14-27 FEBRUARY 1900) WERE TREATED. THE ROYAL ARMY MEDICAL CORPS, COMMANDED BY DR. F. TREVES, WORKED UNDER DIFFICULT CONDITIONS, BUT HAD GOOD EQUIPMENT AND AMPLE SUPPLIES AND WERE PROVIDED WITH COMFORTS BY "THE LADIES OF THE COLONY". THERE WERE FOUR GRASS-FLOORED OPERATING AND DRESSING STATIONS, EACH SURROUNDED BY BELL TENTS WHICH COULD ACCOMMODATE 100 PATIENTS. THE WOUNDED ARRIVED BY TRAIN OR AMBULANCE OR WERE CARRIED HERE BY INDIAN STRETCHER-BEARERS, OFTEN OVER LONG DISTANCES.

National Monuments Council
1988

the line, presumably old railway buildings, and in front a wood shading the little fenced graveyard. Numbers of individual graves and monuments are there but the prime interest for most will be Freddy Roberts' memorial stone marking where he lies. 'Frederick Hugh Sherston Roberts V.C.' The name Sherston may be familiar for Roberts's relative, Colonel

'The position of the General Officer Commanding will be near the 4.7″ guns.' (Orders by Lieutenant-General Sir Francis Clery KCB – number 10.) Buller observing events unfolding from his post on Shooters Hill.

Sherston, was killed at Talana Hill on 20th October 1899, and thus death had struck Lord Roberts and his wife twice in two months, taking nephew and son. 'Bobs' learned of his son's death on the same day that he accepted command of the forces in South Africa, replacing Buller.

But that sad fact is to anticipate the story.

Driving back to the road and going two kilometres further on, Clouston Field of Remembrance is found to the left of the road, on the farm of that name. This is familiar ground for it is on the side of the low hill known to the British as 'Shooter's' where Buller sat with his powerful telescope at the start of the day. Nearby were the famous naval guns and the forward hospitals. These guns were only available at all because of the inventive mind of Captain Percy Scott RN of HMS Terrible *who, when the Boer invasion began, had his ship's guns adapted to land use, mounting them on great timbered gun-carriages. Ladysmith was supplied just in time and the Natal Field Force was equipped as well, but with iron wheeled 4.7s and even a 6″ gun.*

As for the forward hospitals, they were the responsibility of Sir Frederick Treves (1853-1923), one of Queen Victoria's surgeons and a leader in the new field of operating for appendicitis. In 1902 he operated successfully and famously on the King, Edward VII.

There was a Zulu on duty when we were there, issuing an A4 sized

ANGLO-BOER WAR 1899-1902
BATTLE OF COLENSO 15.12.1899
AFTER THE ACTION AT BRYNBELLA ON 23 NOVEMBER 1899 AND THE
BRITISH WITHDRAWAL TO ESTCOURT, THE BOERS UNDER THE COMMAND OF
GEN. LOUIS BOTHA ESTABLISHED A DEFENCE SYSTEM ALONG THE
TUGELA RIVER TO PREVENT THE BRITISH FORCES FROM RAISING THE
SIEGE OF LADYSMITH. IT STRETCHED FROM HLANGWANE TO THE COLENSO
KOPPIES AND THE BEND OF THE TUGELA RIVER. THE BRITISH TROOPS,
COMMANDED BY GEN. REDVERS BULLER, ADVANCED FROM NEAR CHIEVELEY
AND LAUNCHED A THREE-COLUMN ATTACK SUPPORTED BY AN ARTILLERY
BOMBARDMENT. BUT THESE WERE BADLY CO-ORDINATED. FROM CONCEALED
SANGARS AND TRENCHES THE BOERS FIRED ACCURATELY ON THE
BRITISH INFANTRY. THE BRITISH FORCES WERE EVENTUALLY FORCED
TO WITHDRAW AFTER LOSING TEN ARTILLERY PIECES AND
SUFFERING HEAVY LOSSES.
National Monuments Council
1988

Buller's view of the battlefield in front of Colenso. It was from this spot, near the naval guns, that he observed the opening stages as the British troops attempted to cross the Tugela River under heavy fire. *copy of an ordnance survey map of the locality with a plan and explanation of the site. The Garden is a spacious place which seems, to some extent, artificial as the memorials are laid out in what is the start of a system, though the order is incomplete. It is like any other part-filled graveyard. However, if one considers what the thoughtless and destructive 'advance' of commercial progress has cost Britain, here is a worthy attempt to protect the markers erected quickly and respectfully at the scene of battle, when later needs for the use of land have been identified. No doubt the incomplete feel of it all will disappear as the years pass. Many monuments are to do with tragic events in the area later in the campaign.*

Here, or remembered here, are the Royal Inniskilling Fusiliers who died in the 'loop,' as are some of the 2nd Queen's Royal Regiment, Imperial Light Horse, Natal Carbineers, 66th Battery RFA, and other Royal Field Artillerymen. There are some who died after Colenso like the men of the 1st Royal Dragoons, Leicestershire Regiment, Royal Dublin Fusiliers, and Bethune's Mounted Infantry from Tugela Heights. Their are individual graves like those of Captain T. H. Berney and Private W. Brass (2nd West Yorks), Lieutenant C. M. Jenkins (Thorneycroft's Mounted Infantry), Private Webb, Lieutenant Colonel C. C. Thorold and Captain W. L. Thurburn (Royal Fusiliers), Captain

A. H. Goldie and Lieutenant C. B. Schreiber (RFA) and last, but not least, Captain M. L. Hughes (RAMC) who was killed near Buller when riding along the line with his staff. Also there are monuments to the Royal Scots Fusiliers and the 14th and 66th Batteries RFA.

A postscript is provided by Troopers Rainsford and Boshoff, drowned in the Tugela on April 6th, 1904.

From the top of the rise, standing somewhere near where Buller sat and was photographed, the panorama is spread out before us, but again a recurring problem in the area is met. Photography, war artistry and newspaper reporting were all developed or developing by 1899 so there is often a good picture of what the ground looked like. Now it is possible to see how much it has changed. Not the horizon, of course, because that is immutable: Grobelaar Mountain on the left; Umbulwana above Ladysmith in front; Hlangwane to the right and Monte Cristo to the far right. Hlangwane is of interest because on closer inspection it has not changed a deal, as the record shows that the cover offered to the defenders by its scrub worried Buller, and it is scrub-covered now. In spite of changes, natural and urban, before us are the Colenso Kopjes, Fort Wylie and the higher hills of Tugela Heights (Wynne's, Hart's, Railway and Pieter's), opposite the hump of Hlangwane.

Much has changed, however, below the skyline. The loop in the

Colenso Railway Bridge as left by the Boers. The hill in the background is Fort Wylie, which was occupied by Boers during the fighting and gave them a clear view of the attacking British. Museum Dept. of Kwazulu-Natal

River Tugela was not visible to Buller because like many South African water-courses, it flows in the bottom of a gully. However, the ground was evidently sufficiently bare to allow the Commander in Chief to see the Irish Brigade at work, whereas now extensive wooded hedgerows have grown up, screening the flatter land where the river bends. Directly in front Colenso has grown too, even sporting a small two-storied block of flats near the station, much like the ones built in British cities thirty years ago and often now being pulled down. From Clouston or Shooters Hill however, the most obvious change is the cooling towers of the power station built in 1924. This utility, which was a social benefit and has itself now been overtaken by the years, is an unfortunate obstacle to understanding the stages of the battle.

General Buller assembled his staff to explain the plan which was issued in the name of the Assistant Adjutant General. Although its written confirmation did not reach the brigadiers until about midnight they met with their senior officers that evening. Hart made clear to his officers that the 5th Brigade was called upon to make a crossing and attack before the main thrust began.

The written plan is here reproduced as printed in the *The Official History of the War in South Africa*. The 'Iron Bridge' is the Bulwer, or road bridge.

From the same spot today. All that remain are the piers, which were built in the late 1880s.

'Orders by Lieutenant-General Sir Francis Clery K. C. B., Commanding South Natal Field Force. Chieveley.

14th December 1899 10 p.m.

1. The enemy is entrenched in the Kopjes north of Colenso Bridge. One large camp is reported to be near Ladysmith road, about five miles north-west of Colenso. Another large camp is reported in the hills which lie north of the Tugela in a northerly direction from Hlangwane Hill.

2. It is the intention of the General Officer Commanding to force the passage of the Tugela tomorrow.

3. The 5th brigade [Hart] will move from its present camping ground at 4.30 a.m., and march toward Bridle Drift, immediately west of the junction of Doornkop Spruit and the Tugela. The brigade will cross at this point, and after crossing move along the left bank of the river towards the kopjes north of the iron bridge.

4.The 2nd brigade [Hildyard] will move from its present camping ground at 4 a.m., and passing south of the present camping ground of No. 1 and No. 2 Divisional troops, will march in the direction of the iron bridge at Colenso. The brigade will cross at this point and gain possession of the kopjes north of the iron bridge.

5. The 4th brigade [Lyttelton] will advance at 4.30 a.m., to a point between the Bridle Drift and the railway, so that it can support either the 5th or the 2nd brigade.

6. The 6th brigade [Barton] (less a half-battalion escort to baggage) will move at 4 a.m., east of the railway in the direction of Hlangwane Hill to a position where it can protect the right flank of the 2nd brigade, and, if necessary, support it or the mounted troops referred to later as moving towards Hlangwane Hill.

7. The Officer Commanding mounted brigade [Dundonald] will move at 4 a.m., with a force of 1000 men and one battery of no.1 brigade division in the direction of Hlangwane Hill; he will cover the right flank of the general movement, and will endeavour to take up a position on Hlangwane Hill, whence he can enfilade the kopjes north of the iron bridge.

The Officer Commanding mounted troops will also detail two forces of 300 and 500 men to cover the right and left flanks respectively and protect the baggage.

8. The 2nd Brigade division, Royal Field Artillery, will move

at 4.30 a.m., following the 4th brigade, and will take up a position whence it can enfilade the kopjes north of the iron bridge. This brigade division will act on any orders it receives from Major-General Hart.

The six Naval guns (two 4.7in. and four 12-pr.) now in position north of the 4th brigade, will advance on the right of the 2nd brigade division, Royal Field Artillery.

No 1 brigade division, Royal Field Artillery (less one battery detached with the mounted brigade), will move at 3.30 a.m., east of the railway and proceed under cover of the 6th brigade to a point from which it can prepare the crossing for the 2nd brigade.

The six Naval guns now encamped with No. 2 Divisional troops will accompany and act with this brigade division.

9. As soon as the troops mentioned in the preceding paragraphs have moved to their positions, the remaining units and the baggage will be parked in deep formation, facing north, in five separate lines, in rear of to-day's artillery position, the right of each line resting on the railway, but leaving a space of 100 yards between the railway and the right flank of the line.

    In first line (counting from the right) :
        Ammunition column, No. 1 Divisional troops.
        6th brigade Field Hospital.
        4th brigade Field Hospital.
        Pontoon Group, Royal Engineers.
        5th brigade Field Hospital.
        2nd brigade Field Hospital.
      Ammunition column, No. 2 Divisional troops.
    In second line (counting from the right) :-
      Baggage of 6th brigade.
      Baggage of 4th brigade.
      Baggage of 5th brigade.
      Baggage of 2nd brigade.
    In third line (counting from the right) :-
      Baggage of mounted brigade.
      Baggage of No. 1 Divisional troops.
      Baggage of No. 2 Divisional troops.
    In the fourth and fifth lines (counting from the right) :-
Supply columns, in the same order as the Baggage columns
  in second and third lines.

Lieutenant-Colonel J. Reeves, Royal Irish Fusiliers, will

command the whole of the above details.

10. The position of the General Officer Commanding will be near the 4.7″ guns.

The commander Royal Engineers will send two sections 17th Company, Royal Engineers with the 5th brigade, and one section and Headquarters with the 2nd Brigade.

11. Each infantry soldier will carry 150 rounds on his person, the ammunition now carried in the ox wagons being distributed. Infantry greatcoats will be carried in two ox wagons of regimental transport, if Brigadiers so wish; other stores will not be placed in these wagons.

12. The General Officer Commanding 6th brigade will detail a half battalion as Baggage Guard. The two Naval Guns now in position immediately south of Divisional Headquarters camp will move at 5 a.m. to the position now occupied by the 4.7″ guns.

By order

B. Hamilton, Colonel,
Assistant Adjutant General
South Natal Field Force.'

The eighteen guns were commanded by Colonel Long, Officer Commanding all Royal Artillery in Natal, and sited according to Buller's instructions; the other artillery was to the left under Lieutenant Colonel L. W. Parsons, and at rear, near to Buller's HQ, there were the bigger Naval Guns (two 4.7″ guns and four 12 pdrs.). Two 12 pdrs. were on Shooters Hill, near to Buller's HQ on Naval Gun Hill.

At 4.30 am the troops moved up, with all officers having discarded their swords, as ordered, and often therefore carrying identical equipment to the men, and at 5.20 am the 4.7s opened-up from a position 4500 yards from Fort Wylie, without drawing any response. Hart's objective, Bridle Drift, was upstream of a place where the River Tugela turns northward and then back on itself. The result is a 'tongue' shaped piece of land pointing Northwest [the 'Loop']. Hart should not have been in there but his map, it is said, was unclear and he took the lead of his ill-informed guide, who then disappeared. Hart was brave but old-fashioned and, unbelievably, all the men save the first battalion were sent forward in close order. It was now that Botha opened fire because of the threat posed by Long's guns and his signal was obeyed by the defenders opposite the tongue or 'loop,' as well as the rest of the

A company advances in close order. It was in formations such as these that the British moved forward to cross the Tugela River, presenting an unmissable target for the Boers in their concealed postions on the opposite bank.

line in front of the artillery. Effectively the Boers had Hart on three sides and to make matters worse, he dragged in his own left wing under Lieutenant Colonel T. Thackeray [destined to lose his life three months later], who may have been going in the correct direction for Bridle Drift.

The Dublin Fusiliers reached the river but could not cross, and were followed by the ranks of pointless sacrifices urged forward by Hart. According to one observer, a lieutenant in the Connaught Rangers, the river was in flood anyway and the men by the water's edge could from there see that the trenches were marvellously laid out, as near to the water as 120 yards. Not that men were actually in sight, for he only saw three Boers withdrawing at about 2.00 p.m. and others, too, wrote that the ridges across the river appeared to be deserted, the men unable to see the Boer positions, only hearing the ceaseless rattle of musket

See map
on page 49

45

Prior to the Battle of Colenso a tactical meeting (*kriegsraad*) was convened by the Boer commander, Louis Botha.

fire. When they bobbed up to peep, they were shot by their invisible foes. The Irishmen had to lay pinned down by mauser and pompom fire for eight and a half hours, many men seriously wounded and plagued by flies and thirst – and even, in at least one recorded case, dysentery. The 2nd Dublins carried haversacks, water-bottles, rifles and 150 rounds of ammunition: but no great-coats, blankets or mess-tins.

The Royal Inniskilling Fusiliers Museum has in its archive the diary of Private L. J. Bryant who was with the Irish Brigade throughout this period. He writes bluntly about what he has experienced, but without criticism.

'5th December.

"The force struck camp at 2 am, we fell in at 3 am and marched off to the scene of operations, to take up our respective positions. My Regt. is in the 5th or Irish Brigade, along with the Dublin Fusiliers, Connaught Rangers, and the Border Regiment. Our scouts had reported all clear and we were marching along not thinking that the enemy were so near us, and we were marching in Mass of Columns when all of a sudden two shells from the Boers' guns burst amongst our Brigade and our Colonel gave us the order to "Extend" and so we went into action. Our

Brigade formed the left flank of the operations, under the command of Major General Fitzroy Harte [*sic*], and our formation was intended to be as follows; - Firing Line, Dublin Fusiliers and Connaught Rangers; Supports, Border Regt, Reserves, Inniskillings, but the Boers opening fire so suddenly took us all by surprise, so that we had no time to get into our proper formation, so the consequence was all parts of the Brigade were in the Firing Line, altho' we still had our Support and Reserves.

The Boers were intrenched along a high range of Kopjes and they also had trenches dug at the bottom of the Kopjes, and we could not see any of them, as they kept well under cover. Whilst they were practically safe in their trenches, we had no cover at all as we were on level ground, so making a good mark for the enemy, and they took good advantage of it too and made things very hot for us.

Members of a Boer Commando, tsypical of those who held at bay an army of the greatest empire the world had seen.

The Tugela River flows between the Boers' Position and us, and they had dammed the River and also put barbed wire entanglements in the river just under the surface, so that if we tried to cross we would get entangled in with wire and so be shot down or else drowned. The fight lasted about nine hours, and although we advanced up to the water's edge we could not cross it, and so had to retire. The losses on the British side were very heavy, amounting to about 1200 casualties. Our regiment's losses were 19 killed and 97 wounded, not counting prisoners, which however were very small. Our side also lost 10 guns which fell into the hands of the enemy, altho' a plucky and daring attempt was made to recover them, but the Boers opened a terrific fire on the Gunners and they had to give up the attempt, though not before they had done as much as any mortal man could do.

Shortly after the battle was over, the Boers robbed our dead. We retired back to Chieveley again and reached our camp for the night.'

Now, as you peer forward from Buller's position 'the loop' is not distinguishable in any way due to the woodland and scrub that have sprung up in the twentieth century, and moving forward will show that

The Dublins attempt to cross the River Tugela and pay the price.

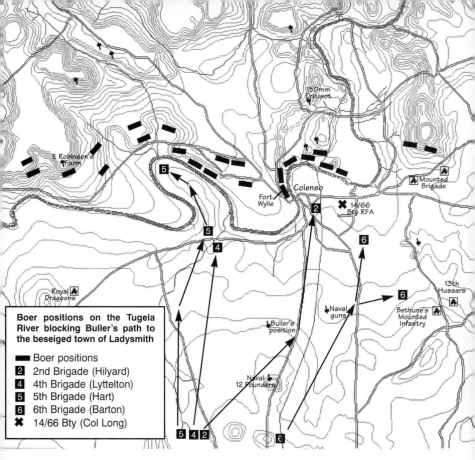

Boer positions on the Tugela River blocking Buller's path to the beseiged town of Ladysmith

- ▬ Boer positions
- **2** 2nd Brigade (Hilyard)
- **4** 4th Brigade (Lyttelton)
- **5** 5th Brigade (Hart)
- **6** 6th Brigade (Barton)
- ✖ 14/66 Bty (Col Long)

it is on private land. It is possible to enter some way into it to visit the *Ambleside Military Cemetery*, where the Irishmen who died are interred, and the way do this is to **leave Colenso for Winterton** and **turn right** on the dirt road, opposite where the R74 comes in from Greytown. This back road also goes to Winterton, and more directly, and after approximately a thousand yards is the little bridge known as Kitchener Bridge, and the cemetery is down the track to the right.

The best view of the loop, though, is to be had by crossing the Tugela and going up the main Ladysmith Road. As you get near the top of the hill, pull off the road and look back. It is easily traceable from here by the trees and verdant vegetation following the river's meandering.

All was peaceful silence opposite the British right. In due course Long, a veteran of the Afghan War of 1879-1880 who had seen famous action at Omdurman in '98, had marched the twelve guns of the 14th and 66th batteries up to about 900 yards from the river and began to

The Irish Brigade in the 'Loop', shot to pieces but still attempting to cross the river.

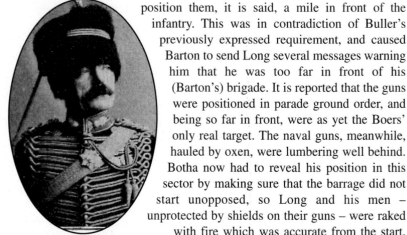

position them, it is said, a mile in front of the infantry. This was in contradiction of Buller's previously expressed requirement, and caused Barton to send Long several messages warning him that he was too far in front of his (Barton's) brigade. It is reported that the guns were positioned in parade ground order, and being so far in front, were as yet the Boers' only real target. The naval guns, meanwhile, hauled by oxen, were lumbering well behind. Botha now had to reveal his position in this sector by making sure that the barrage did not start unopposed, so Long and his men – unprotected by shields on their guns – were raked with fire which was accurate from the start, as the Boers had taken the precaution of white-washing the railway fence and nearby rocks to Long's left as a range-finding device.

Colonel Long who sited his guns (14th and 66th batteries) too far forward and under observation and fire from Fort Wylie.

The artillery was not doing well against the entrenched Boers and now Hart was trapped and the shells from the British left-hand guns were falling among the leading troops. On the right, Barton's Royal Scots Fusiliers ran short of ammunition, new supplies being brought under heavy fire by Sergeant Major J. Shannon (2nd Royal Irish Fusiliers).

At 7.00 am Buller was aware that the guns were where they should not have been, and to make matters worse Long, his assistant and other officers were casualties. The men performed well, but at the end of an hour they had lost twelve gunners dead and twenty-nine wounded and had taken cover in a dry river-bed. The Boer fire was reduced but the attackers were by then down to 4 men per gun. The guns and ammunition were left unattended, reproaching Colonel Long for his choice of position, while the Naval contingent was still struggling with the ox teams to get their heavy guns into position. The gunners showed unbelievable bravery as the ammunition began to run out but they were forced to take shelter where Buller found them when he went down there himself. He ordered Lieutenant Ogilvy RN to retire his naval guns to Captain Jones. This was done one by one, covered by 'C' squadron, 13th Hussars. Ogilvy had three men wounded and 28 oxen killed, wounded or lost.

Out on the far right Dundonald's men were about a mile from Hlangwane when he ordered them at 7.15 am to continue on foot and

Looking into the Loop towards Ambleside and the Irish Brigade graves from Kitchener Bridge on the dirt road from Colenso to Winterton (Springfield). Hart took his men in close order into this death trap, even drawing in Lieutenant-Colonel Thackeray's section which had been in the correct place up stream.

View of the Loop from the heights on the Colenso-Ladysmith road across the river. British guns were shelling this ground believing the Boer guns to be situated on the high ground. In reality they were lower down and close to the river. The tree line in the distance indicates the Loop which the Irish Brigade entered.

Roberts is hit while trying to save the guns.

A gun from 66 Battery. The crew are said to be the men who served at Colenso, therefore one of them is Corporal (later Second Lieutenant) Nurse.

in open order. He met ferocious resistance but made some progress, and he was encouraged to think that, with the assistance of infantry, he could take the hill. He requested support from Barton but that General applied his mandate quite literally and refused to commit any men to the enterprise.

From his vantage point Buller had seen all this and sometime after 7.00 o'clock he instructed Lyttelton to get 5 Brigade out. Lyttelton responded by moving men up (two battalions says one writer, but four companies of the Rifle Brigade, says another) across the mouth of the loop to cover the withdrawal.

However, this was difficult due to the excellence of the enemy fire. The next month, when the Boers made a determined attack on Platrand (Wagon Hill and Caesar's Camp) at Ladysmith, the British were the defenders and had laid down the new invention of telephone lines, which served them well. Here, however, being the attacker and therefore mobile, the Commanding Officer had no messenger save the ancient one of the galloper, now seen to be in desparate need of replacement due to the quality of modern fire-power. The communication with company officers was slow and highly dangerous, and the messenger sent to Hart went forward to the very front, where he cut into the middle of the Irish line, rather than arriving at the right-hand end, as he believed. He informed only the people to

The markers of 66 and 14 batteries make a great arc beyond the road. Here the last of 66 battery are in view. Freddie Robert's marker (inset), which is actually to the right and off the main view.

Soldiers of the Durham Light Infantry provide covering fire for the attackers as they seek to disengage from the abortive British assault on the Boer positions.

his left, who withdrew, leaving the right-hand portion in place, where they suffered heavy loss. Eventually the 5th Brigade struggled out through Lyttelton's 4th Brigade ninety minutes or so after the advance began. And, again, the artillery wrongly shelled them. Nearly all were rescued but at 3.00 p.m. Thackeray and his troops were invited to surrender to a group of Boers who had swum over and cut them off. They managed to extricate themselves.

Hart's casualties here were 532, forty per cent of them being Dublin Fusiliers.

Henry Hildyard, Commander of the 2nd Brigade, was now leading his men in a way familiar to them, though they had never seen active service together. The brigade had come directly from Aldershot where, already under Hildyard's command and under the direct gaze of Sir Redvers Buller, they had trained together. In open order the Devons, Queen's, East Surreys and West Yorks were launched straight at the little town of Colenso itself. They took the town and punished the Boers across the river so hard that they forced them out of the lower trenches. This should have been the cue for the naval guns to hammer the exposed mass of men, but the gunners could not be sure that they were not the brigade itself and, yet again, the British misunderstood the moment. A common error in this war, it seems.

*Follow Hildyard down the road **into Colenso** itself, a further 2.5 km. The 'Official Municipal Brochure' reminds us that the town was named after Bishop John William Colenso. He was an interesting and controversial figure who, although Bishop of Natal, was excommunicated in 1860 for heresy – he floated the idea that parts of the Bible were not to be seen as literal – only to be reinstated by the Privy Council. He was a great friend to his native parishioners and having called down odium upon himself for his views of scripture, he later brought to the notice of the Colonial Secretary, Lord Carnarvon, the facts of the atrocities visited upon the Hlubi and Putini people in the mid-1870s by the settlers in the so-called rebellion led by Chief Langalibalele. Again he was excoriated by his fellow whites. The authorities misled him into thinking that they would act in the best interests of the natives, but after the British defeat at Isandlwana, 22nd January 1879, he knew that he had been badly used by them.*

According to the Municipal Brochure the town had been named back in 1855 though there were but forty-two names in its Directory in 1908. It must have been a very small place in 1899, and is tucked into another loop in the river, spreading south away from it. The Bulwer Bridge connecting Durban with Ladysmith and beyond is just one lane wide and can have changed little since it was built in 1879, the year of the Zulu War battles of Isandlwana, Rorke's Drift and Ulundi. To cross it the battlefield visitor must follow the road round at right angles to his line of travel and stop to check that there is no traffic facing him. Of course, this can be avoided by staying on the R74 and missing the town altogether, but battlefield visitors would not want to do that. Colenso became a township in 1926 and a borough in 1958. The growth of town has obscured that part of the field on which Hildyard was operating more successfully that his colleagues, but the continued existence of the Bulwer Bridge on his left front and the railway line on his right flank help to clarify it. Certainly the little toll house at the bridge was there at the time and now houses the very interesting Robert Elliot Stephenson Museum exhibiting photographs, maps and military artefacts lost at Colenso or Tugela Heights and brought here to rest. Ask for the key at the Police Station next door, where it will be signed out to you.

Hildyard's brigade comes out of this story with credit and it was to him that Buller turned for help with his gunnery problem, which haunted him to the end of his days. He arranged for that officer to send men to cover the guns with heavy rifle-fire.

Dundonald away on your far right meanwhile needed a lead from Buller, but Buller was otherwise engaged. He was now in the hollow to the rear of the guns, surrounded by wounded men. Deciding that he could not cross the river without guns, he concluded that withdrawal was his only option – after saving the guns. They were still in the open and represented sitting targets for the mausers across the river. One historian reports that there were wagons full of ammunition with them, but in Sir Redvers Buller's report to the Royal Commission into the War in South Africa he tells how, when on his way to determine the cause of the artillery's silence, he met two officers from the batteries who told him that they had fired away nearly all their ammunition. Once there Buller came to his momentous decision, and stopped all further attempts to sustain the action.

He is said to have stood in the open in full view of the sharpshooters and shouted for volunteers to save the guns.

A series of efforts were made to recover the guns under heavy fire and two were brought out but the second attempt cost, it is said, seven out of 13 men, including Lieutenant Freddie Roberts who was shot three times; and 13 out of 22 horses. The men struggled back to the donga and Major William Babtie CMG of the Royal Army Medical Corps who had already shown great bravery, along with Captain Congreve [later to be a Corps Commander in the Great War], brought Roberts into shelter.

In the donga with the gunners was Lieutenant Colonel G. M. Bullock with other men from the Second Battalion the Devon Regiment, when the Boers appeared, having swum across the Tugela. An argument about surrender ensued in which Bullock was hit in the face with a gun-butt. At this the men capitulated, the wounded being released to the British stretcher-bearers.

Seven Victoria Crosses were awarded to men in this sector; Captain W. N. Congreve [whose son won one, posthumously, in 1916], Rifle Brigade; Captain H. L. Reed, 7th Battery RFA; Capt. H. N. Schofield, RFA, one of Buller's ADCs.; Corporal G. E. Nurse, 66th Battery; Private C. Ravenhill, Royal Scots Fusiliers, Major W. Baptie CMG RAMC and Lieutenant the Hon F. H. S. Roberts, KRRC (posthumous).

Lieutenant S. G. Francis of the 2nd West Yorkshire Regiment wrote home from near Colenso on December 17th,

'Unluckily a Field Battery got badly hammered, and could not be got out of action. They were blown to pieces by the big guns of the enemy and we were unable to help them. No officers and only a few men came out of it.'

At Colenso six Victoria Crosses were won, apart from the Hon F.H.S. Roberts' postumous award. From the top and clockwise: Captain (later Lieutenant-General) Congreve; Corporal (later Second Lieutenant) Nurse; Captain (later Lieutenant Colonel) Schofield; Major (later Lieutenant-General) Baptie; Captain (later Major-General) Reed; Private (later plain Mr) Ravenhill.

Of his own Brigade's attack he wrote,

'although some of the leading companies got across the river, they could not get up the hills beyond. The position was much too strong for us, and we could not have carried it without terrible losses...We succeeded in getting a very good idea of their position, which we had not got before, but I cannot help thinking that we were meant to take the position, which we failed to do. Our losses were very heavy, amounting, I believe, to over 1000.'

He had been assigned to Hildyard for the day as a galloper, and his despondency revealed in the foregoing quotes still leaves room for his admiration of, or maybe frustration with, the senior officers:

'One of the most risky things I saw, was Buller going from one flank to the other. He had a huge staff, and General Clery with his staff was with him, and when he came to us, Hildyard and his staff chipped in, and we rode right across the front, being shelled all the time – but I think only an orderly was hit – how no more were I cannot understand.'

Another of that regiment who was close to the Commander in Chief for a time was Private W. Sykes and he confided in his diary,

'Buller was against ['near?'] me with all his staff and he looked in a bad way at the loss of so many men...'

Buller then rode back to the Mission Station between Advance Hill and Hussar Hill to confer with both Dundonald, who thought that with one or two battalions of infantry he could take Hlangwane, and with General Barton, who thought that his whole Brigade would be needed. Redvers Buller's opinion was that the hill was only of advantage if he was across the Tugela so Dundonald was told to hold on, whilst Barton retired.

On the way back through the men, he decided that they were suffering so badly from heat and could be in heavy fighting after dark, so he left the guns where they were and returned to camp. Out of over 19,000 men present, the day had cost 1139 casualties, 143 of whom were dead. For the Boers seven were killed and about 20 wounded.

Drive into town 'behind Hildyard' *through the belt of bungalows like those in Winterton, looking for the Central Restaurant and Cafe, and opposite this* **turn right** *along West Street. This is an anonymous side-street and in front, across the end, is the railway line, still very much in use. You are forced right at the T-junction and* **follow the road** *round* **over the railway** *by an arched bridge.*

Across the line you are at the front of Barton's sector, for here is where Long sited his guns. Nothing in the scene is as expected from the story, but driving down the railway-arch the road curves to the right round a raised piece of grassland. Here **turn off** *and walk into a series of concrete blocks arranged in a long line. These mark the sites of the guns of the 66th and 14th batteries, Royal Field Artillery, although they may well have been moved back some yards when the power station was built.*

It is sad that vandalism has been a regular feature of the battlefield memorials over a number of years, and this place has suffered with

others. There is a marker showing the spot where Freddie Roberts fell which had recently been vandalized, and the guide who kindly assisted the writer to find the guns in October 1996 told him that he had reported the act recently. Creditably the authorities had replaced the plaque quickly. Who could do this? In front of us, some distance away far beyond the line of the guns, is a township and an immediate answer could be that black youths who have no stake in this part of South Africa's history may be to blame. This could be too glib, however, as the same problems exist in Ladysmith and we were told by local people there that white youth is involved. Also, a plate commemorating something as historically noteworthy as this may have some perverse interest to a rogue collector, but it can scarcely be of any use in a local living-room of any colour.

Standing in line with the guns, where the men would have been, the donga is to the rear, and, once into its shelter, only a very brave man would voluntarily climb out. And yet they did, into the shot and shell to hook the guns up again to their horses. One rarely thinks of the way in which horses have no part in deciding when and how they work, but here in this story it strikes forcibly how fearful it would be for them too. To recover the guns Buller asked for volunteers and it was another sad conspiracy of chance and unforeseen occurrence that the son of his supplanter should be on hand; a volunteer, and mortally wounded. Louis Botha is said to have commented on the terrible scene as the gunners struggled while a hail of fire poured down upon them. He had wanted to look away but could not do so, being riveted to the horror that his men were creating. As already noted, Buller himself was dealt a painful blow by a spent shell and later his surgeon was blown to bits beside him.

To apply these historical facts to the geography, which is one of our purposes in being there, is not easy. Imagination is needed to overcome the depredations caused by mid-20th century modernity which now, to add a mordant twist to the situation, has itself lapsed into obsolescence. The track on which you have driven continues past the gun-sites and bears right to the township and into a more bushed area towards Green Hill and Cingolo. To the left, back the way you came, is the railway line where great changes have been made. The map of the field as at 11.00 o'clock shows that as you stand by the position of the guns, to your left and right is where the Scottish Fusiliers were, two companies on each side. Immediately behind you were two companies of the Royal Irish Fusiliers, and to their rear, one body behind the other, were the Kings Royal Rifles, then the Devons, and at the rear the

East Surreys. This important railway line is like any such in England, with a clutter of lineside features added over the years making a confused industrial mish-mash of concrete, steel and other materials. Cables, wires and assorted equipment are mounted on these supports, contending that modern railways everywhere need this ugly litter to live and breath. You are at the approach to Colenso Station, a much bigger and more untidy affair taking up a greater length of track than would be the one that the soldiers and Boers saw. It was new in 1888 and the surrounds would be much less cluttered in 1899 than they are now. Today it would not be possible for the defenders to simply whitewash the fence and rocks to assist their range-finding.

Then the greatest change is, of course, the view forward. Stand up where Freddie Roberts was hit, and looking to the front, note that you are on a slight rise, with the lane from the railway-arch in front of you at a rather lower level, and snaking away right towards the distant township. Beyond it is the railway embankment leading to the Power Station compound. The two cooling towers are tiny compared to the ones at home but the view is all but obscured and it is hard to judge how near to the enemy Colonel Long was. By climbing up the redundant embankment, now denuded of lines, one can stare down the yard between the buildings and see the hump of Fort Wylie. It seems very near. What is easy to picture is the donga behind us filled with sheltering and wounded men with Buller making his own examination. Even twentieth century progress has not entirely obliterated the scene of the tragedy.

On the 16th, Assistant General Louis Botha, creator of the defence lines, and, therefore, the victor of Colenso, sent the following telegram (National Army Museum 6412-11 No 81, Translations of Boer Telegrams) to the Transvaal State Secretary in Pretoria:

'15.12.99 The God of our forefathers gave us today a brilliant victory. We have repulsed the enemy on all sides at three different points. We allowed them under a heavy bombardment on their side to bring 12 cannons to the river, and, as soon as their horses were unhooked we opened fire with mausers and killed their assistants and shot them out of position to such an extent that they only succeeded in getting two cannons back. We took the other ten beautiful large cannons with 13 filled ammunition wagons. We have taken prisoners about 150 of their best men who so bravely stormed time after time. Among them are several officers. The enemy's loss must have been terrible.

They are lying on one another and I think quite 2000 men. On our side about 30 wounded and dead. I will send you a correct report later on about this. I can with a thankful heart congratulate you and the Africander people on this brilliant victory. I am compelled to insist that the British Government must understand that under the sheltering mantle of the Red Cross the cannons seek positions or protection as they did all over, and at one place three times, and once the cannons were actually permitted in this manner to get through the river. I respectfully request the Government to appoint a General day of prayer to thank Him who gave us the victory.

– ends.'

'Our Africanders.'

That was how the Boer commander saw it, and much has been written about how the British leaders viewed things.

What of the rank and file? There still exists a great deal of material in diaries and letters home, written by other ranks and filled with the details of army life – trivia and hardships alike. Many of them give the lie to the popular idea that Tommy Atkins was illiterate but one writer who shows a low degree of literacy is Drummer Goodwin of the 2nd West Yorks. Some of his statements are incorrect, punctuation is almost absent and the spelling is improbable to say the least, also his hearing and memory of senior officers' names is faulty. Nevertheless, his seeming lack of schooling prevents him from using the over-stuffed prose that some of the educated would use, and he has a grasp of detail. His story is fascinating and no criticism of authority comes through. The lack of punctuation adds to the flavour of the sequence of events tumbling into disaster. Consider this:

'The Division struck camp at 3 am the order for Parade was given. To parade at 5.00 am to advance to Colenso to try & drive the enemy out of his position so that we could relieve Ladysmith. The Division was told of as follows The Irish Brigade under Command of General Hart on the right flank. The English Brigade under command of General Hilyard centre and the Scotch Brigade under the command of General Littlehorn on the left flank & in command of the Division General Cleary & Commanding operations (General Sir Revers Buller) & and that there was the mounted troops commanded by Lord Wundonald consisting as follows South African Light Horse, Imperial Light Horse Infantry, Colonel Scouts, 13th Hussars Bethuna Mounted Infantry then the Artillery consisting of the (66th 63rd) 7th 14th 19th 28th 78th. Batteries of Royal and Field Artillery & eight

Naval Guns and then there was a reserve Brigade under Command & General Barton consisting of the Kings Royal Rifles Essex Regt, the Division advanced in fine stile some of the boys singing & some pasing jokes but when we came in sight of Colenso it looked a terrible position the hills are terrable hight & we had nothing but a long plain to go over & they were well in their trenches our Naval Guns started shelling the enemy & our artillary & Infantry moved forward under the fire from the Navals. The Artillary came into action & then the Battle got nicely hot the enemy firing their big guns into our Infantry who were still advancing & getting a terrable fire from the enemy but were sticking it well & the sun came out & it was terrable hot & no water & the 66th of 63rd Battaries then moved to a better position as the Officer thought but it turned out a trap for they had not unlimbered when the Pom Pom's & Rifle fire mowed them down & they were forced to leave the Guns but they tried like men or Iron to get them back but both men and horses were mowed down as fast as they went to try & get them back but they managed to get 2 guns out of twelve back and the Infantry had got to the river & some of the lads trying to swim accross, but it was lined all over with barbed wire so many of the brave lads got drowned then came the order to retire, where we lost more retiring than advancing & we retired out to Chievley reaching camp about 4.30 our losses being 1311 killed 9 wounded & 10 Artillery guns & we got an issue of rum at night and then laid down to rest for the night.'

Poor lad...and poor Buller. Now other means had to be found to relieve Ladysmith.

The road bridge over the Tugela, opened in 1879 and named after Sir H.E.G. Bulwer, Lieutenant-Governor of the Colony of Natal. His Boundary Commission of 1878 found largely for the Zulu and was infamously neutralised by Sir H.E. Bartle Frere, British High Commissoner at that time.

Chapter Three

SPION KOP
23th - 24th January 1900

Just for a few months the town of Springfield (now known as Winterton) was important in the lives of British working men; at least those who had chosen to be working for Her Majesty and had been brought here on the instructions of the War Minister.

What they found was a very small agricultural centre at a crossing over the River Little Tugela, most of the inhabitants of which today are Zulu, with a small white population. Many of the white townsmen dwell in good sized bungalows set in sweet gardens, and the two main roads to Colenso, (one becomes a reasonable dirt road in dry weather, but enquire locally; the other is a good blacktop) begin their exit by being lined with these pleasant homes that now only exist in England in the Austin, Rover and Morris Catalogues of the twenties and thirties. There is a mill which grumbles night and day, save for Sundays; two filling stations, grocery stores, and a clothes shop. A cafe, a photo-developers and a bank are there; a stationers, a haberdashers, material shops and a butchers are on the main street; a laundromat, B&Bs and a very comfortable little hotel, 'The Bridge,' with its related wine, beer and liquor store will all satisfy the visitor's needs.

Altogether attractive now and in warm weather, but what of January

The British view of Spion Kop, taken from the Winterton (née Springfield) to Potgieter's Drift road, the R600.

*1900, fresh from the setback of Colenso? We must remember that even
though often shrouded in haze, the Drakensberg are a few short miles
away and we should keep in mind that the heat of Natal's summer days
can contrast sharply with the bitterness of her nights. The parched
condition of the land can quickly change to sodden muddiness.*

The Diary of the 2nd Battalion, Lancashire Fusiliers makes
interesting reading and gives the flavour of a Natal Summer as tasted
by an Infantryman:

'Dec 24, 1899. Arrived Estcourt by 4 trains from Durban.

Dec 26th - 31st. Practiced attack formations daily, furnished
outposts round Estcourt. Very heavy rain daily. Have 6
Regimental transport wagons.

Jan 9, 1900. Camp struck and marched to Frere Camp at 5 am
in very heavy rain. arr. 3.45 pm due to five hour delay at flooded
drift.

Jan 10th. Fine morning allowing time to dry out kit. Struck
camp at 12 noon, marched at 3 p.m. for Springfield. Halted for
tea approx two miles from Frere. Heavy rain at 7 pm; roads very
heavy. Left at 7.30; very slow.

Jan 11th. Marched until 3.00 am; halted until 5 am, reached
Pretorius Farm at 7.30 am. Breakfast. Left at 11 am for
Springfield Bridge which reached at 1.30 p.m.. Served as
advance guard. Bivouacked near bridge until dusk when moved
and pitched camp in dark, finishing at 9.30 p.m.'

The 1st Battalion, South Lancashire Regiment had a similar
experience when we consider the record in the diary kept by 3582
Lance-Corporal C. Bradley of 'H' Company. On that same morning of
the 9th of January he was awakened by Reveille at 3.00 am and they
struck camp in pouring rain at 3.30, breakfasted at 4.00 and then were
ordered to march at 5 o'clock; apart from 'H' Company who were on
baggage guard and stood in place until 11 o'clock. The roads were, he
says, at least a foot deep in slush and water: it never stopped raining
and all the men's greatcoats were in the wagons.

They arrived at Frere at 4.00 pm, ate dinner and tea together with a
'peg' of rum before laying down for the night in the open and just as
they were. The next morning, the tenth, they marched on in mud and
rain, even fording a river at waist depth.

On the eleventh the sun came out and 'nearly flattened us out as we
could not get any water', respite only coming when the same dinner-
tea combination was taken. The same arrangement, that is, as the night

before, followed and with a repeat of the breakfast menu as well, hard biscuits and bully-beef.

General Buller had now been joined by the 5th Division, commanded by Lieutenant-General Sir Charles Warren, a man with as much personality and as colourful a past as the Commander-in-Chief himself. When much younger Warren was responsible for the remodelling of the defences at Gibraltar. He then turned to archaeology and led the way in the excavation of Jerusalem, finding Hezekiah's Tunnel (the king of Judah in the eighth century BC who constructed an underground water course to ensure supplies in the event of a siege) and having his name left there in the title 'Warren's Shaft.' In 1884 he commanded a body of irregulars in successfully occupying Bechuana-land, though he could not handle the bullying Rhodes. He then briefly left the army and had less success in charge of New Scotland Yard where Jack the Ripper eluded him. Buller welcomed his arrival and sent him straight to work.

The Commander-in-Chief's dispatch after Spion

Lieutenant-General Sir Charles Warren, KCMG, arrived in time for the move upstream to the Potgieters Drift area. His artillery, shown below moving up from Frere Camp.

Kop said of Lieutenant-General Warren's march towards Springfield from Frere:

'Torrents of rainfall on the 9th (January) filled the spruits, and indeed rendered many of them impassable for many hours. To forward supplies alone took 650 ox wagons and as in the sixteen miles from Frere to Springfield there were three places at which all the wagons had to be double-spanned, and some required three spans, some idea may be formed of the difficulties; but these were all successfully overcome by the willing labour of the troops.'

Springfield was then a tiny place, but the bridge over the Little Tugela was already there, and is still. Hence, no doubt, the name of the Hotel.

Back to the Lancashire Fusiliers' Diary again;

'Jan 13th. Field Order issued by Sir R. Buller read to Battalion on parade:

Field Order – Springfield 12th January 1900

The Field Force is now advancing to the relief of Ladysmith where, surrounded by superior forces, our comrades have gallantly defended themselves for the past ten weeks. The General Commanding knows that everyone in this force feels, as he does, that we must be successful. We shall be stoutly opposed by a clever, unscrupulous enemy. Let no man allow himself to be deceived by them. If a white flag is displayed, it means nothing unless the force displaying it halt, throw down their arms, and throw up their hands at the same time. If they get a chance, the enemy will try and mislead us by false words of command and false bugle sounds. Everyone must be on guard against being deceived by such conduct. Above all, if any are ever surprised by a sudden volley at close quarters, let there be no hesitation; do not turn from it, but rush at it – that is the road to victory and safety. A retreat is fatal. The one thing the enemy cannot stand is our being at close quarters to them. We are fighting for the health and safety of our comrades; we are fighting in defence of our flag against an enemy who has forced war upon us for the worst and lowest motives, by treachery, conspiracy and deceit. Let us bear ourselves as our cause deserves.

By order,
(signed) A. Wynne,
Colonel Chief of Staff
Jan 14th-15th. Usual camp routine'

Spearman's Military Cemetery. Thornycroft's Mounted Infantry's gravestones can be seen here clearly on both photographs, which are diagonally opposite to one another. The evening light obscures the flimsy crosses of the shilling-per-day regular rankers. Above, the explanatory slab is centre rear right and the Spearman family are in the railed section to the left.

The Highways Department have made things very convenient for the visitor to Spioenkop. Today, leaving Winterton on the R74, the Bergville Road, the options are to turn right on to the R600 immediately Winterton's little 'built-up' area finishes, or to stay on the R74 to Bergville (21 km), then turn right on the R23 (also called R616 on Tourist Maps), for the dirt road up to the top of the Kop. By the latter route the visitor has also turned the Boers' flank, as did Dundonald, and Acton Homes is seen to be a tiny little community indeed, with a native General Store beside the road. Both roads meet 10 km from Ladysmith so the whole massif is skirted by road and a good picture can easily be formed. What has changed is that a dam has been constructed at the foot of the ramparts, putting Trichardt's Drift under vast volumes of water and the reservoir is girt with the Spioenkop Nature Reserve. Neither of these features in any way spoils the visit: in fact, the visitor can be well served by the nature reserve, as if your companions are more easily bored by battlefields, an interesting alternative day can be spent viewing the animals. Days even, for reasonably-priced campsites and cabins are available – right under the brow of the battlefield and opposite Buller's HQ on Mount Alice. A bonus is a good Battlefield Display in the Reserve's Visitor Centre.

In the writer's view it is preferable to start with the R600 route so as to take in the size of the problem presented to the British generals.

To reconnoitre one can go that way in the evening and within ten km or so of Winterton, some time before the Nature Reserve, and before the Ladysmith road plunges down to what was Potgieter's Drift, a sign is reached which directs the visitor to Spearman's Military Cemetery and also Mount Alice Farm. The latter is private property and the house is surrounded by an electrified fence, but in the tea-time light the writer parked past the farmhouse and went into the cemetery. There is a black slab with the Crown insignia at its head and underneath:

VR

No 4 Stationary Field Hospital
Spearman's Farm
January-February 1900
Here lie many of the brave British Soldiers
who died of wounds received in the actions at
Spion Kop and Vaal Krantz most of whom spent
their last hours in the nearby hospital
Sir Frederick Treves who was consulting surgeon
has related much of what happened here in his
"Tale of a Field Hospital."

At the end nearest the farm buildings, under the trees, are the last resting places of the Spearmans, G. Spearman 1889; his wife Susan 1883. When Treves was here that was all, but beside them are now George Spearman, 6th November 1938, and Anna Spearman 1881-1973. Treves's comments in his 'Tale' are well made; the monuments 'are fitly carved... and distinctly the product of no mean town,... and yet inappropriate of the lonely graves at the foot of the kopje.'

In joining the older couple, George and Anna were also associated with the remains of British officers and private soldiers alike, who ended their days so far from London or Middlesex or Lancashire or Scotland or South Yorkshire. The writer wondered about Privates J. Mallin, J. Toole, W. Strachan of the York and Lancs, his own local regiment, but others may, no doubt, find home links of their own. Another interesting point, here as elsewhere, is that the men of Thorneycroft's Mounted Infantry all seem to have headstones of a uniform pattern. So do those of the other ranks of the regular regiments, but they are simply worked up from flat steel bar, whereas Thorneycrofts' are quite well-finished in stone.

Evening is a good time to wander round this plot, as the cows are coming home, and the cries of the Zulu cow-herds and the lowing of the cattle helps the whole atmosphere to be outside of any particular time, either a 'then' or a 'now.'

Private J Toole
York and Lancaster
Regiment
Killed in Spion Kop action

The visitor is brought down from the philosophical to the corporeal by struggling up the kopje to the crest, probably believing at first that this is Mount Alice. It is not, of course, because the usual deception of such hills is at work, and from the top

View from the top of Spearman's towards Spion Kop.

Spioenkop's lip can be seen peeping over Mount Alice a long walk in front. Depending on the weather when visited, make some judgement of the private soldier's difficulties due to being cold and soaking wet and often sleeping in the rain, or being burned black by the great heat of the sun. There is the problem of hygiene, with the lavatorial arrangements for thousands of men too awful to contemplate, and the spasmodic opportunities to wash clothes and bodies alike. For your part, all you have to do is look to your footing and follow the story.

Find a suitable place to stop further along the R600 and survey the whole succession of cliffs and hills across the River Tugela and see the immensity of Buller's problem. Away to the west the Drakensberg

See map on page 33

marches down the land and dwarfs everything, but it is a coy giant, and often hides its face in haze or cloud-wreaths. Turning round to the right is the lower ground by Bergville and the other road to Ladysmith, via Acton Homes, before the Tugela defence lines start properly with the mass of Rangeworthy Hills, also known in the accounts as Tabanyama, but seemingly properly called Ntabamnyama. Turning further the eyes are drawn on, over the reservoir and Nature Reserve, where Warren's HQ and Three Tree Hill are in front of the great mass, and then there is Spioenkop itself, like the back of a stranded sea-creature. On its top is what appears to be a tower, but is actually a prominent and impudent tree, and only when viewed through binoculars can the monuments to the fallen be clearly picked out. Right again and the ridge is seen to fall to a saddle before tilting up to Twin Peaks. Mount Alice may now be in the way, but across the R600, almost at our back, is Vaal Krantz and further away, invisible also from here, Doornkop and Onderbrook which played their parts in the besting of Buller the month before.

On January 16th Buller's force crossed the Tugela. Lieutenant-General Sir Charles Warren's camp at Springfield was left up, tents erected and bodies of troops wandering about, with normal bugle calls being sounded in the hope that the soldiers who had moved out in the night would escape the notice of Boer observers. The men had one day's rations and 150 rounds, and were carrying waterproof sheets. No talking or smoking was allowed. Three miles out a change of direction told the men that Trichardt's, and not Potgieter's, was the objective.

The first men over the river were 1st Rifle Brigade, 2nd Scottish Rifles and 61st howitzer battery.

The General's brief was to break through west of Spioenkop or 'Lookout Hill', as Buller intended that he should cross over Ntabamnyama, believing that Botha would not be ready. Warren has been accused of dillying and dallying without properly preparing, and on the night of the 21st the 2nd Lancashire Fusiliers, the 2nd Devons, the 1st York and Lancs, the Border Regiment and the Royal Inniskilling Fusiliers occupied the crest of Ntabamnyama.

The 2nd Battalion, Lancashire Fusiliers recorded events:

'Jan 16th. Left Springfield at 5 p.m. and marched to a point above Wagon Drift on the Tugela, which we reached about 12.30 am and bivouacked.

Jan 17th. Wet night and left at 8.00 am, crossed pontoon bridge before occupying ridge covering bridge.

Jan 18th. Boers seen to be preparing position in front. Heavy firing all afternoon on our right, presumably by Lyttleton's Brigade at Potgieter's.

Jan 19th. Battery began to shell Boers. Bivouacked at Coventry's Farm.

Jan 20th. Formed for attack about 1 p.m. on right of York and Lancs. Advanced against Boer position but could not take main one. Heavy, accurate fire. Battalion lost 15 NCOs and men killed; 123 wounded including 7 officers. No food. Bivouacked on field. Battalion attached to Hart's Brigade.

Jan 21st. Up at 4 am and under fire, then moved to left as second line of attack.

Jan 22nd. Held hills round front and left flank of valley all day. "Pretty heavy fire," especially towards evening. Relieved by 2nd Devons after dark and bivouacked in valley.'

Several historians have criticized General Warren's activities here and it is difficult for a layman to understand who was right, he or Buller, in the controversy that was to break later on. In the event, after taking time to make up his mind, **Warren deliberately assaulted Spion Kop itself**, believing that its precipitous sides would cause the Boers to think it impregnable. If the attack was successful he thought he would dominate the road north and would have an ideal site for heavy artillery. However, Lieutenant Colonel Blomfield, who commanded the Lancashire Fusiliers on the kopje wrote in a piece which appeared in the *Annual of*

Lieutenant-Colonel Charles J Blomfield DSO

This was the view from Conical Hill as the Boer marksmen saw it. Boer riflemen held Twin Peaks until the afternoon. They were firing from Aloe Knoll all day.

the 2nd Lancashire Fusiliers for 1900,

'My own view is that the position was always absolutely untenable. The top of the mountain was evidently small and very exposed to the north, to which it sloped downwards. Had our guns ever been got up they would not have remained in action ten minutes.'

The problem facing the British General has been seen, and the hardships suffered by their men, and now it will be necessary to go to the 'Boer' side of the range in order to visit the battlefield and get an overview of the British position. To do this either return to the junction of the R600 and R74, and turn right, turning right again at Bergville along the R23/R616; or **proceed further along the R600**, **over the bridge** *that replaces Potgieter's and on towards Ladysmith, but where the* **road joins the R616 turn left** *away from Ladysmith and go back* **down the R616**. *For the sake of this narrative, it is assumed that the British position was visited on one day, and the Kop on the next.*

A visit can take as many hours as you wish, for this is a haunting and spectacular place besides a graveyard and memorial. In view of the climate, visitors should know that there are no refreshments available on the summit of Spioenkop. Water, certainly, should be taken.

From Winterton to Bergville is, as was said earlier, 21 kilometres and after turning right onto the R616 **proceed a further 24km** *or so before coming to the sign, (to the right, of course from this direction),* **'Spioenkop 11km.'** *That figure is accurate. The countryside is totally*

Spion Kop

Spion Kop summit and the far side were held by the British. The near face and, from about midday, the near crest of Spion Kop was held by the Boers.

*different from the River Tugela side of the hills, with, as the accounts tell us, the land sweeping away in a far gentler descent to the plain behind. This is now a dirt road that is perfectly adequate, at least in the fair weather that we have seen, and as the first section went through Zulu farm land, we encountered a tractor, broken down and spread in the road, with a grinning boy in charge. A little negotiating and we could grin back and continue. The road turns out to be very steep at one point, with speed humps at regular intervals, so progress is slow as it winds up with **Conical Hill** above on the left and Green Hill*

The view from Spion Kop looking towards Conical Hill and the Boer positions below the summit.

Conical Hill

dominating the right. At the top is a small carpark with a sole attendant who charged R5 for the entrance and had a descriptive booklet for R3.50 and a self-guided trail map for R1.50. A small tip will be graciously received, and, as we had been promised in Winterton that we should have the summit to ourselves, and indeed we did, the trail-guide was an excellent idea. In truth, to be there alone is a privilege. [However, better to come prepared with this book, as sometimes the attendant is not to be seen until you leave, when he dutifully asks for the toll.]

Before leaving the carpark area it is as well to look around. Evidently this is on the top, but not at the top, for the actual summit rises more or less regularly to around the area of the main British Memorial, and then gently falls again past the end of the Lancashire Fusiliers' trench before sweeping down a saddle to Twin Peaks in front, or falling to the Tugela at right front. Of course, because of the domed summit this is hidden from the carpark.

See map on page 33 *Spion Kop's situation is best understood from the top, and to the south will be seen the River Tugela and the Reservoir in the foreground, and Spearman's Kop beyond beside Mount Alice, where Buller was; sweeping right is Springfield (Winterton) and the road down to Frere, Estcourt and Ulundi. Trichardt's Drift is to the right, but out of sight below the water. Next and to the north is Ntabamnyama, with, behind, the green of Acton Homes settlement and beyond the backdrop is the wall of the Drakensberg from Giant's Castle in the south past Mont aux Sources to Majuba Hill in the north.*

You are now looking north-eastwards to east, over a rolling plain with the heights around Ladysmith in the background; Caesar's Camp, Umbulwana and so on. Their background is the Biggarsberg, round to Impati, beneath which stands Dundee. Lastly face east to south-east and see nearer to you Twin Peaks, Vaal Krantz, Doornkop and Onderbrook to the muddle of the Heights of Tugela, Hlangwane etc.

From the left, or north of your position, a flat ridge becomes Green Hill, reaching out to Ntabamnyama. In front is the slighly lower Aloe Knoll and to the right Twin Peaks.

Those who ascend to the top are thus almost looking down on everyone else in an arc round them, but from a totally exposed position themselves. *The Times History* makes the point in its account,

'...(a) balloon, rising to a height of 2000' commanded a view of the summit and northern slopes quite sufficient for the construction of a sketch serviceable for tactical purposes. But no such sketch was ever made, and neither Sir C. Warren nor any of

76

the officers who took part in the operation had more than the vaguest idea of the shape of the mountain they were to occupy.'

Before leaving the car park 'base' it should noted that there is a litter bin and also well-constructed and well-hidden toilets here, let into the edge of the scarp, facing Green Hill and Ntambmnyama.

At the car park we are on part of the forward position that Major-General E. R. P. Woodgate adopted soon after 7.00 am, but to get the story in the correct order you are directed to walk to the right, (right, that is, with your back to Ntabamnyama). In front there unfolds a view of a spur falling out and down from Spioenkop towards the dam. Below is where Warren's HQ was.

Early on 24th January, **Woodgate was ordered to take the peak of Spion Kop**. It appears that Warren attempted to impress on him that the British should only entrench and occupy the rear crest of the summit as they were doing on Ntabamnyama. They would be out of range of Boer artillery and the Boers would have been exposed on the top to British shrapnel as they pushed forward. This seems, however, to deny the possibility of mounting big guns safely on the summit.

The Lancashire Fusiliers again:

'Jan 23rd. In the morning rejoined XIth Brigade. Paraded for night attack on Spion Kop at 7.30 pm. Attacking column consisted of 2nd Lancs Fusiliers, 4th Kings Own (six companies), two companies South Lancashire Regiment, Thorneycroft's Mounted Infantry, half a company of R.E. and Volunteer ambulance. Marched all night.'

In a letter home to a Mr. Peacock on January 29th, Corporal Walter Herbert of The King's Own wrote,

'at 8 p.m. Tuesday we were marched off into the dark (literally and metaphorically) to we knew-not-where. At about 12 midnight we reached the foot of a tremendous looking hill, but not looking half as tremendous as it really was – as after climbing one spur we found another awaiting for us and then another... an uncomfortable feeling took possession of me as I remembered it was the anniversary of Majuba.'

The Lancashire Fusiliers:

'Jan 24th. Climbed Spion Kop and were fired on by piquet, which we rushed, and then occupied hill. Misty and dark; entrenched ourselves. Sniping soon began and as mist cleared shell-fire commenced. Under extremely heavy fire until 8.00 pm when it was decided that the position was untenable and the force retired.'

Six companies of the 2nd Battalion The King's Own Royal Lancaster Regiment marching in column, and at ease, towards Spion Kop.

As Corporal Herbert of the Royal Lancasters continued to Mr. Peacock,

> 'The mystery is how any of us escaped. And what was it all for? None of us know though probably you in England know from the papers.'

In England they had no more idea than Tommy Atkins had.

Lieutenant Colonel Blomfield wrote in his own account,

> 'On the 23rd the Battalion returned (with much thankfulness) to its own Brigade (the XI.). At midday Major-General Sir E. Woodgate sent for me, and said that Spion Kop was to be taken that night, and that as he "must have tried troops" for such a hazardous operation, he had determined that the Lancashire Fusiliers should lead the way.

> At 3.40 pm I received the following orders from the Brigade Major:

> (1) The G. O. C. has decided to seize Spion Kop this night.
> (2) The following troops will compose the force:
>> Royal Lancaster Regiment (6 companies),
>> 2nd Lancashire Fusiliers.
>> 110 of Thorneycroft's M. I. [Mounted Infantry]
>> Half Company of 37th Company R. E.
> (3) The above troops will rendezvous at White's Farm, about 1/2 mile N. E. of Pontoon Bridge, at 7 pm
> (4) Extra ammunition will be carried on the mules supplied by the 10th Brigade.
> (5) One day's complete rations to be carried. Wagons with supplies of great coats will be brought up as soon as possible without exposure; also water carts and machine guns.
> (6) The S. Lan. Regt. will hand over six mules, 3 to each Battalion, for water carrying purposes.[sic]
> (7) Pack mules will be utilized for carrying water in water-proof sheets.
> (8) 20 picks and 20 shovels to be carried in regulation stretchers.
> (9) Password, "Waterloo."

With regard to these orders, No 3 was modified later, and the rendezvous changed to a spot north of White's Farm.

> Order no 7 was quite impossible of fulfilment [sic], waterproof sheets being useless as waterbags, and biscuit tins were tried as improvised water tanks. They were not a success.

The steep climb up the mountain tilted the boxes to all sorts of angles, and though the tops were covered with wood and canvas, there was not much water left when the climb was done.

At dusk we moved off from the bivouac we had been on for the afternoon of the rendezvous, reaching it about 8.30 p.m.

Here we met the rest of the column and two companies of the S. Lancashire Regiment sent to reinforce the six companies of the Royal Lancaster Regiment. There was some discussion as to who should lead the column, and finally Lieutenant-Colonel Thorneycroft was selected for this most difficult and responsible undertaking of leading some 1,600 men up an unknown mountain on a dark night, against a determined enemy of unknown strength.

Colonel Thorneycroft had seen the eastern side of Spion Kop and also the western side of it, and was thus the best available man to lead us up the southern slopes.

There were, I believe, two native guides told off for this march, but one bolted, and the other was incompetent.

The order of march was thus arranged:

Thorneycroft's M. I. (about 15 officers and 120 men).

The Lancashire Fusiliers.

Six Companies the Royal Lancaster Regt.

Modern view of General Woodgate's approach up Spion Kop, with colonel Thorneycroft acting as Pilot – night of 23rd/24th January.

Two Companies the South Lancashire Regt.

Half Company 27th Company R. E.

Mules, etc.

General Woodgate marched at the head of the Lancashire Fusiliers. Colonel Thorneycroft led the column, assisted by Captain Brunker, 2nd Lancashire Fusiliers.

It was an extremely dark night, though the stars gave a faint light when the drizzling rain permitted. The track on which we moved across the valley to the west of the spurs running down from Spion Kop to the Tugela was narrow and undefined, and single file was frequently necessary. Constant halts had to be made to let the column close up. Once across the valley the upward climb began, and though a broader front could now be used, there was nothing but the vague loom of the mountain to the north to guide the stumbling footsteps of the column. Here the skill and resource of Colonel Thorneycroft became apparent. He would halt the column and go on alone for one or two hundred yards to feel for a way on, and then come back and lead us forward. About a third of the way up a Kaffir kraal was passed about 11 o'clock, and we knew that so far all was well, and that we had worked up to the end of the lowest of the three slopes that form the southern approach to Spion Kop. This kraal was one of the few landmarks there were.'

A. W. Thorneycroft was a major in the Royal Scots Fusiliers who had raised the corps known as Thorneycroft's Mounted Infantry and they had been engaged since November. Thorneycroft quickly surveyed the route and made notes of the key features, hence he was assigned to lead the way.

Blomfield continues,

'The higher the column climbed, the thicker was the mist. What little wind there was blew in our faces, and well it was for us that it was so, for sound sleeper as the Boer is, the noise of nailed boots on rocks must have wakened some of them had we been up-wind of their posts.

Slowly, but surely, we clambered up, and now we were on a plateau that surely must be the top. The Battalion was at this time in four successive lines, or double companies, with 100 yards or so between the companies, and men in single rank. [At times the climb was so steep that they had to use their hands] Suddenly a hoarse voice from the left front shouted, "Wi kom dar," and immediately a heavy, but ill-directed fire was opened in our direction. Obedient to the orders previously issued, every man threw himself flat on the ground till the fire slackened, and then on the word "Charge," the Battalion dashed forward, cheering and holloaing, and Spion Kop was ours. Lieutenant Awdry bayoneted a burly Dutchman in a trench, and a few others were killed, as they fired at us from behind the rocks; but except these, all the garrison, from 80 to 100 strong, dropped down over the mountain side by paths and tracks they knew by heart and awaited developments.'

Captain CH Hicks, killed on Spion Kop. Son of Hicks Pasha, who was killed by the Mahdi 1883,

You are now above the spur, and the approach certainly looks steep. I think I could have managed it, but in a long time, and the noise of heavy breathing would give me away. It would be hard to do so in silence even for young men. There is the usual dishonest series of false hopes before you. They can be seen with hindsight, but the climber would repeatedly think he was at the top, only for another sneaky incline to be revealed.

Herbert continues,

'After 5 hours climbing we were nearing the top when without a moment's warning we got a volley blanked fairly into us from a short distance it was pitch dark so you can understand that there was near being a panic but after a moment the boys recovered themselves and fixing bayonets made a dash and the hill was ours.'

The place is marked, 'In memory of an unknown Burgher sentry killed on this spot.' It is hard to find an account which names the British soldier who killed the burgher, other than Lieutenant Colonel Blomfield's, but from him we learn that it was Lieutenant Awdry, who later in the day was killed himself.

Blomfield:

'I ascertained afterwards that this little Boer garrison had been for three weeks on Spion Kop before we crossed the Tugela, so they had ample time to make themselves acquainted with every nook and cranny of the mountain top. The mist was so thick that it was impossible to signal down by lamp

Captain V H A Awdry

to the camp that the orders of the G.O.C. had been carried out, but resounding cheers bore the news to the anxious watchers down below.'

General Warren would thus know that the objective was theirs, allowing him to commence artillery fire on the nek between Green Hill and Spion Kop, as well as the reverse slope. No attempt was made to determine the extent and shape of the summit.

On a magnificent Natal day, such as the writer has experienced, a good evaluation of the surroundings can be made, but it is vital to remember the situation that Woodgate and his men were in, with the summit obscured by mist. Lieutenant Colonel Blomfield will have something to say about this in a little while.

The first evidence of warfare that is seen today is the start of the pathetic attempt at self protection. The wall is at first broken down but visible, then the whitewashed stones arc away so that the men's backs, if they could have turned round and looked, were towards Spearman's and their camp. They curve up the hill and are interrupted by the South Lancashire Regiment's Monument, and nearby a double grave with the name Tr. C. Sleigh, 5th Lancers, and also another name superimposed, but much weathered over the years. The Regimental Memorial says that it is, 'In memory of the undermentioned Officers, N.C.Officers and men of the 1st Battalion South Lancashire Regiment who fell on Spioenkop on 24th January 1900' *and lists a captain, a lieutenant, two sergeants, two lance-corporals and six privates.*

Sandbags had been forgotten, though the Royal Engineers had shared out between the men shovels, picks and some crowbars so at 4 o'clock Major Massey and his sappers began to tape out a curved, 200-yard trench line on what was believed to be the crest. (The notes in the 'Self-guided Trail' say 400 metres.)

As the visitor walks up towards the South Lancashire Memorial, he is following the line of that original trench.

The Queen's Lancashire Regiment has in its possession a document written by a member of one of the two companies of South Lancashire Regiment who must have been in this section. His words say,

'A heavy rifle fire and everybody made for cover such as it was, there being only one long trench... it was about 8.00 by this time, about this time the enemy had commenced a terrible cannon fire, we could not get any big guns on our hill to reply it was about this time Major General Woodgate was hit with a

'The first evidence of warfare that is seen today is the start of the pathetic attempt at self protectection...' It will be noted that the field is naked and the men were completely exposed... 'the wall is at first broken down and visible, and the white-washed stones arc away up the slight slope.'

piece of bursting shell and severely wounded the next to go was Capt. Virtue [sic] our Brigade Major who met with an instantaneous Death. The Rank and File fell freely, it was about this time that our Brave Capt fell (Capt Birch) he being about two yards from me at the time a bullet passed through his head, Death being instantaneous the next to fall was our brave Lieut Raphael by this [time] groans and moans of the wounded was terrible and the most pitiful sight. All crying for water and stretcher bearers but none could be found. The morning passed away everyone thinking his time had come, early in the afternoon we was reinforced by the I.L.I. Middlesex and Scottish Rifles which gave us a little heart we still fought on a losing game. By this time the trenches was full of Dead and Wounded and at last Darkness came it was then the welcome order came for everyone to retire on the Field Hospital. The order by Colonel Thorneycroft who was then in command, arrived at the Field Hos (sic) about midnight, myself and Sergeant Price bivouacing together.'

The trench made an arc, roughly facing Ladysmith, of course, with fifty yards behind it a rocky outcrop, but at its right-hand end two curved sangars only had to do. Many tools had been dropped on the hill, and the sandbags left at the bottom, so the trench was a poor shallow affair, scratched out with entrenching tools in rocky soil. The rocks were piled into a wall a foot or eighteen inches high, infilled with debris. At about 6.30 the men could have a rest. All being shrouded in cloud, no-one knew that the right-hand end would turn out to be in enfilade from Aloe Knoll, 250 yards to the right. On the right were the Lancashire Fusiliers, on the left the Royal Lancasters and South Lancashires, and in the middle Thorneycroft's Mounted Infantry. Woodgate sent Colonel Repington `a Court, Buller's staff officer attached, back down the hill to Warren to ask for naval guns, and to inform him that he felt himself to be secure, but 'fog is too thick to see.'

At 7.00 am the error of their position was understood and troops were sent forward to occupy new positions at the northern edge, and, briefly, between 7.30 and 7.45 the British had a view of 'their hill.'

These new positions at their left hand end by the carpark have

86

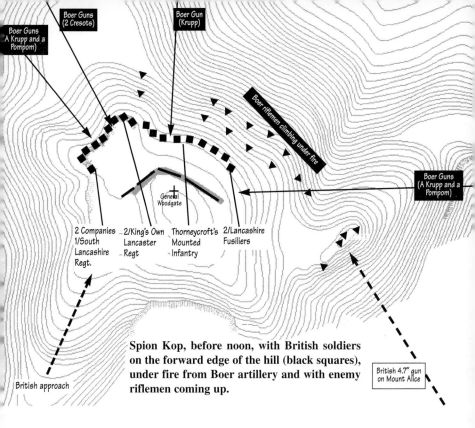

Boer Guns
(2 Cresots)

Boer Gun
(Krupp)

Boer Guns
A Krupp and a
Pompom)

Boer riflemen climbing under fire

Boer Guns
(A Krupp and a
Pompom)

General
Woodgate

2 Companies
1/South
Lancashire
Regt.

2/King's Own
Lancaster
Regt

Thorneycroft's
Mounted
Infantry

2/Lancashire
Fusiliers

Spion Kop, before noon, with British soldiers
on the forward edge of the hill (black squares),
under fire from Boer artillery and with enemy
riflemen coming up.

British 4.7" gun
on Mount Alice

British approach

already been walked and now the tour is on the opposite flank towards
the end of the trail. Roughly in the middle is the Boer memorial.

Meanwhile, General Schalk Burger's men were beginning to retire,
pack up and leave but Botha moved in to strengthen the Boers' resolve
and he brought up artillery at close range with two other guns three
miles away; two of them were 6˝ Long Toms on the rear slope of Green
Hill. According to the trail-guide there were five field-guns and two
pompoms. The ninety-odd strong Carolina Commando under Henrik
Prinsloo was assigned to storm the ridge and ascended to a line
between Conical Hill and Aloe Knoll, Spion Kop's outliers.

Corporal Herbert again;

'about 6 a.m. we were under the hottest fire from about 8,000
rifles that I ever hope to be under, but even that was not the
worst. Shortly their Nordenfelt started barking...TA says it says
'buck up! buck up' and really it is not unlike it, except that it
makes one buck down pretty sharp when he hears it and for the
next 16 hours our noses were buried in the ground except when
we were firing.'

Whether his recollection of timing or his opinion of the numbers of enemy guns is correct or not, when the mist cleared he and his comrades were seen to be in a death-trap.

Various illustrations, including the one on the cover of the trail-guide, and the tiled mural from the Transvalia Theatre entitled 'Spionskop' suggest that there is a great eminence nearby overlooking the hill. There is not. The top is a crown and from the South Lancashire end, the left, you cannot see the Lancashire Fusiliers end, near as it is – especially when prone. Standing up would be madness, for Ntabamnyama, Green Hill, and Twin Peaks are rather laid-back but with the nearer Conical Hill and Aloe Knoll all are so placed as to expose any man on the summit in outline, as naked as on the day he was born. Once the mist was burned off there was no hiding place, apart from the pitiable little wall that the soldiers had thrown up.

The mist cleared by 8.00 am and the Boers were revealed, clambering up the hill. As they neared the top the soldiers hit them hard, but the defenders were themselves under fire from Conical Hill and Aloe Knoll and the attackers got a foothold. The British retired to their main trench already knowing that it was wrongly placed and they had to hide behind their rocky breastwork while they and the Boers

The right hand leg (eastern end) of the trench of death. Thorneycroft's Mounted Infantry and Lancashire Fusiliers were killed in this section and the shallow trench became their grave.

baked in the sun. Those on the forward crest were exposed to a cross-fire from Green Hill as well as from Aloe Knoll, and the Lancashire Fusiliers, on the right, aiming at the men in their front, were unprotected against the enemy on Aloe Knoll; in fact Botha claimed that 70 of the corpses in the trenches had bullet wounds through the right side of the head.

Boer artillery was now firing from a number of points, as shown in the maps, and was controlled by heliograph and signallers.

Lieutenant-Colonel Blomfield wrote,

'about 8.30 a.m. I noticed a large party of Boers coming along a path, and reported accordingly to General Woodgate. He came back with me to the spot from which I had been on the look-out, and as we were watching the path the General was shot through the head above the right eye.'

A rather more ornate cross says, *'near this spot Major Gen Edward R P Woodgate KCMG CB fell mortally wounded Jan 24 R I P'*; the tiny Lancashire Fusiliers trench is to the right of it as you face the enemy. Facing, and yet if a glance is made to the right and the foregoing is considered Botha's comment is well understood. And all around, as you lift your eyes, is the magnificent view away into the haze towards Ladysmith. The effect of the 'crown' of the hill is obvious and, while the tops of Aloe Knoll and Twin Peaks are all slightly lower than Spioenkop, it is impossible to stress too much that the curvature of the kopje exposes the defenders totally to anyone on those outer peaks.

Major-General E R P Woodgate KCMG, CB

Blomfield again,

'I went to Colonel Crofton, commanding the Royal Lancaster Regiment, the senior officer present, and told him what had happened. As he was now in command, I asked him if there were any special orders for the Battalion, and he said, No, but that he should signal down to say that we were "hard pressed and needed reinforcements." I have a very distinct recollection of the actual words used, and as this message became afterwards of considerable importance, it is as well to record the proposed wording of it.' (sic)

How was it possible in view of the storm of bullets and shells that Mr. Blomfield 'went to Colonel Crofton'? But he did, and there is highlighted what remarkably brave men these

Colonel Croften

were who had to move about on this exposed hill.

Crofton quickly decided that the trenches were wrongly sited and too shallow and that the defensive perimeter was too small. Meanwhile, at 9.00 am Repington `a Court reached Warren and was still upbeat about the situation as his news was from very early that morning, but even then he could report on the shortage of water, indicating what a problem it would be later in the day. At 9.10 am General Coke on Three Tree Hill was told to send another battalion to the summit and the Imperial Light Infantry were assigned to the job, but they initially went too far round the mountain and so wasted an hour.

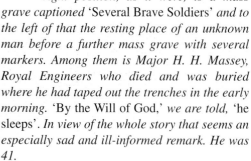

At the rear of the far right of the Lancashire Fusiliers trench is the [Duke of Cambridge's Own] Middlesex Regiment's Memorial 'To the memory of 4 Officers 38 NCOs and men of the 2nd Battn (D.C.O.) Middlesex Regiment who fell at the battle of Spion Kop and are buried near this spot.' *At the inside end of that trench is one* 'In Memory of Officers NCOs and Men of 2nd Lancashire Fusiliers who fell in action 24/1/00' *Then there are a number of private memorials to young men who died that day. If the Lancashire Fusiliers position is the right-wing of the main trench line, then the inside-right position, as it were, is a mass grave captioned* 'Several Brave Soldiers' *and to the left of that the resting place of an unknown man before a further mass grave with several markers. Among them is Major H. H. Massey, Royal Engineers who died and was buried where he had taped out the trenches in the early morning.* 'By the Will of God,' *we are told,* 'he sleeps'. *In view of the whole story that seems an especially sad and ill-informed remark. He was 41.*

General J Talbot Coke

Corporal Herbert's letter continued,

'Shells are a terrible thing to have whizzing over one but a confounded sight worse to have bursting close to ones head as dozens did that day. One man within a few

90

feet behind me was blown to pieces by one and the trenches were soon filled with dead and wounded. The mystery is how any of us escaped.'

Lieutenant Colonel Blomfield unknowingly agreed as he wrote at more length,

'In the centre of the hill top the Sergt.-Major (Moss) was busy serving out ammunition boxes to the trenches. The fire was now very heavy, as 4 of the field guns taken from us at Colenso on Dec.15th, and a Creuzot (sic) 94 pr., had got our range from a sheltered position on the N.W. Nearly every shot they fired took its toll in killed or wounded.

I well remember one shell that hit some men lying in a row behind some rocks that afforded protection to their front only.

'There is no need to dwell on the horrors of shell fire. They must be seen to be believed.' Lieutenant Colonel Blomfield.

The British morning, after the nightmare before.

Two shells passed through the thighs of one man, and on through the legs of the man next to him, leaving only the trunk of the first and carrying away one leg of the second man. A sergeant of the R.E. was lying on the near side of the two men killed and I noticed that his canteen was glittering in the sun, and possibly drawing fire. I told him to turn it round out of sight. The sergeant looked at me, but never spoke or moved, merely turning his eyes towards me, and I learned afterwards that this unfortunate N.C.O. had also been hit by this shell, which had touched his spine and completely paralyzed him.

There is no need to dwell on the horrors of shell fire. They must be seen to be believed.'

Others concurred as, for example, Lance-Corporal Ellison of the 2nd West Yorkshire Regiment who was not on Spion Kop, but was injured at Colenso and repatriated. He arrived home in late March wearing his best red coat, and in a brougham provided from the station. Some of his letters home having been published as news items, he now gave a full account of his activities and said of being under shell-fire,

'There is no man, neither war correspondent nor artist, can describe what an action really is.'

He recounted an instance when one soldier had his head blown off by a shell, and the decapitated trunk remained erect until a sergeant went and pushed it over.

Presumably Corporal Herbert was in the section of trench to the left of the main Memorial and that obelisk is at the left-hand side of the grave containing Major Massey's remains. On its several faces there are listed the names of the fallen: 59 of the Kings Own Royal Lancasters on one face, the commanding General, Royal Engineers, Natal Volunteer Ambulance Corps and Capt. Vertue of the Buffs: 9 men on another, 90 of the Lancashire Fusiliers on a third, 41 of Thorneycroft's Mounted Infantry on another, 37 Scottish Rifles on another, and 42 of the Middlesex Regiment on the last.

Crofton's message that immediate reinforcements were called for was received by Sir. C. Warren at 9.50. Of him *The Times History* said,

'That he could assist... with the 10,000 men at his disposal and in touch with the enemy along four miles of front, was a thing that, even now, he could not or would not see. The suggestion that something should be done on the left seems to have been pressed more than once in the course of the morning by junior Staff officers... beyond some vague discussion with Clery and Hildyard, neither of whom seems to have had the least inclination to do anything, nothing came of it.'

At 10.00 am Lyttelton sent the Scottish Rifles and two squadrons of Bethune's MI against Twin Peaks. Eight naval 12 pounders and two howitzers on Maconochie Kopjes (lower hills above and on the Spion Kop side of Potgeiter's Drift) opened fire on the eastern slopes of Spion Kop where the Boers were now under the lip of the summit and on Aloe Knoll, along with the two naval 4.7s on Mount Alice. Warren sent to Buller and Lyttelton, 'We occupy the whole summit and I fear you are shelling us seriously; cannot you turn your guns on the enemy's guns?'

Thorneycroft's and Colour Sergeant Nolan's (South Lancashires) 'No Surrender!' incident. The artist has clearly used his license, but not too much in view of the small area contested. See page 98.

The sheer poverty of the British defence can be clearly seen from this photograph.

The east end of the trench line. Lancashire Fusiliers with Twin Peaks in the distance and Aloe Knoll in the centre. The ornamental cross on the left marks the spot where Woodgate fell.

Lieutenant Colonel Blomfield:

'About 10.30 a.m. I was walking up to "C" Company's trench, when I was hit by a Mauser bullet through the right shoulder and knocked over. Major Tidswell and Sergeant Lightfoot, of "C" Company, in their trench some 30 yards off, saw me fall, and at once ran out in the most gallant manner and dragged me under cover into their trench. There I remained for the rest of the day.'

Thorneycroft, who had driven off that first picket, was the hero of the piece and now he led a charge in impossible circumstances, only to fall with a twisted ankle under the lattice of fire. Crofton's message to Warren that Woodgate was dead got the response from Sir Charles that help was on the way but it was essential to hold out. Buller could see all this in the distance from his HQ on Mount Alice but only learned after the event that Warren, instead of calling for help from Hart on his left, had received two infantry battalions and a body of mounted soldiers from Lyttelton. Buller is said not to have been consulted but at this distance in time it is impossible to get to the minute by minute truth and pointless, it would seem, to take a position on the matter. Buller was told by Repington `a Court on his return that big guns were

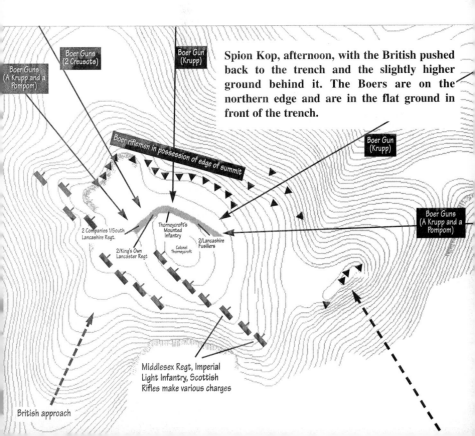

Spion Kop, afternoon, with the British pushed back to the trench and the slightly higher ground behind it. The Boers are on the northern edge and are in the flat ground in front of the trench.

Boer Guns (2 Creusots)

Boer Gun (Krupp)

Boer Guns (A Krupp and a Pompom)

Boer riflemen in possession of edge of summit

Boer Gun (Krupp)

Boer Guns (A Krupp and a Pompom)

2 Companies 1/South Lancashire Regt.

Thorneycroft's Mounted Infantry

2/Lancashire Fusiliers

2/King's Own Lancaster Regt

Colonel Thorneycroft

Middlesex Regt, Imperial Light Infantry, Scottish Rifles make various charges

British approach

called for and the two naval guns were dispatched.

At 11.40 am Buller could see Thorneycroft's valiant efforts from his own command post and he instructed Warren to tell Thorneycroft to take command, which instruction was received on the hillside at 11.50 am. In fact, Thorneycroft was not told until afternoon, by which time he was the only officer left in the front trench.

He was a very large and lively man and led the troops all day with great energy. He was served less than generously by some reports for the way he concluded the battle but he held the action together throughout the day. His report read,

> 'The Boers closed in at the right and centre. Some men of mixed regiments at the right end of the trench got up and put up their hands; three or four Boers came out and signalled their comrades to advance. I was the only officer in the trench on the left, and I got up and shouted to the leader of the Boers that I was the commandant and that there was no surrender. [*This is said to have been about 1.05 pm.*] In order not to get mixed up in any discussion I called on all the men to follow me, and retired to some rocks further back. The Boers opened a heavy fire on us. On reaching the rocks I saw a company of the Middlesex Regiment advancing. I collected them up to the rocks, and ordered all to advance again. This the men did, and we reoccupied the trench and crestline in front. As the companies of the Middlesex arrived I pushed them on to reinforce, and was able to hold the whole line again. The men on the left of our defence, who were detached at some distance from the trench, had held their ground. The Imperial Light Infantry reinforced this part.'

About two o'clock a similar scene was enacted on the left of the British line where the South Lancashire men, behind their particularly pathetic defences, were swamped by a rush of Boers and some caused to surrender. Again, one man broke the spell and it was Colour-Sergeant Nolan who cried out, 'When I surrender, it will be my dead body,' driving the invaders back behind their own rocks and recovering his comrades to their senses.

At the far right of the line is the Monument to the 'Uitlander troops of the Imperial Light Infantry,' *and near here were the Middlesex men. It was here that the Boer attempt to take the British from the side was thwarted by the later reinforcements which included the ILI. It will be remembered that the Middlesex Regiment's Memorial is at the right hand end and to the rear of the Lancashire Fusiliers' trench-grave.*

Buller watches the fight on Spion Kop from a Maxim machine gun position. The photograph on page 65 was taken beside the road below and to the left of this position.

Men from the 2nd Middlesex Regiment had been on their way since 6.0 am and while on the way up had passed General Woodgate on a stretcher going to die. He was part of a procession of wounded, wrote a Private Putland, who said that the wounded told him and his comrades that it was worse than a slaughter-house on the summit. Immediately on reaching the top they ran into a hail of fire when their first casualties were taken including Corporal Clements.

Blomfield:

'About 2 pm two companies of the Middlesex Regiment, and a little later two of the Scottish Rifles, came up to reinforce. They behaved with the greatest courage and energy, but their presence on the top of the mountain merely increased the density of the living target at which the Boers were firing, and their gallant exertions were in vain. They had to withdraw after suffering terribly heavy losses.

It was while the Middles (sic) were fighting that an odd incident occurred. Our men and the Boers apparently advanced simultaneously, both thinking the others were surrendering. After much shouting, and neither showing any signs of giving in, firing was again opened at pistol shot range, and the casualties over this incident must have been extremely heavy.'

99

Private Putland's account is in the diary he kept, now in the possession of the National Army Museum, Reference 8107-18. He too described the maxims as "Buck-up" and he wrote graphically if not grammatically.

'The Boers know the exact distance and consequently the shells fall all around us. Here was where the Lancashire Fusiliers were retiring but after being reinforced by us they come back again to the firing line, they have lost all their officers and had no one in charge of them that caused there (sic) retirement, a tremendous fire met us now and dead, wounded and dying was awful and the groaning was sickening. I was lying on the ground firing with the remainder on the extreme right of the firing line when Captain Muriel told us to go about 60 yards to our right front and about thirty of us went, 2 or 3 of us getting hit there, and directly we got in position Colour Sergeant Morris was... telling me where to fire, he was hit through the nose. He was my right hand man, and directly after this a young fellow was shot on my left. Soon after this I was ordered to go to the main body with a message, as it was not safe to lift your head up off the ground I did not like the job, but I had to do it and there was little time for thinking, so I said a prayer to myself and off I went. The bullets was like rain around me, it was a terrible time for me, and there was any amount of dead here by this time, and the shouts was fearful. While I was doing this Captain Muriel was shot dead after being fairly riddled with bullets.'

The British control of the crest-line was now long gone and this position had become the Boer front-line with the Burghers tucked under the northern edge. They were, as one of their own said, near enough to have tossed a biscuit into their opponent's line.

Talk of left and right or front and rear is almost inappropriate, for the whole field is approximately 650 paces by 350 paces, as paced out by the writer and that could equate to roughly 540 yards by 290. The National Parks Board's leaflet says that the trenches were 400 metres long which equals 437 yards. The section which comprises the three mass 'trench' graves, where a biscuit would have landed, must have been packed with men in a hideous mixture of dead, alive and maimed. Several of the individual memorials attest that their subject was 'killed near this spot,' from General Woodgate downwards, but a number just say 'killed in action on Spion Kop,' and some, British and Boer alike, are 'a brave Burgher' or 'a brave British Soldier,' unknown.

Gradually the ground in front of the main trench became the point of the dispute and it was here where Thorneycroft threw the enemy back by the force of his personality and, as he retired, he met the Middlesex, the Imperial Light Infantry, some Bethune's and the Cameronians, all of whom were ushered into the fight. Again, it is impossible, considering the postage-stamp-size of the field, to understand how anyone was left alive, Briton or Boer.

Men on both sides were taken prisoner and some escaped again so that Putland said,

> '[Our] men that escaped told us that every Rifleman had two or more rifles and while they were firing one, Boys was reloading the others and they also said their killed and wounded must have been close to 3000.'

The British were having a bad time, as we have seen, but what of the Boers? A youngster who had a famous future was Deneys Reitz, son of the Transvaal's State Secretary and he found, as he climbed the hill behind the Boer counter-attack, that there were many dead on the hill-side. Once they had gained the rim of the summit the British trench

The wounded come down from the hill. Somewhere in this procession of pain was Mr Ghandi, leader of Indian stretcher bearers and future leader of Indian millions.

was, he says, twenty yards away, and the effects of the British rifle-fire was causing heavy casualties among them and demoralizing them. Little did they know of the charnel-house at the other side of the dry-stone wall. During the day the dreadful fire-storm and the noise of the artillery wore them down and they began to drift away back down the hill.

Going back to 4.00 pm Warren received the following note, sent at 2.30 but passed through the hands of Major-General J. Talbot Coke who was on the side of the hill and nominally in charge, though he never went to the top. It will be seen that Coke supported the request for more help but insisted, without checking, that the British were holding their own.

'Spion Kop,
24th January 1900 2.30 p.m.
To Sir. C. Warren

Hung on till last extremity with old force. Some of Middlesex here now and I hear Dorsets are coming up, but force really inadequate to hold such a large perimeter. The enemy's guns on north-west sweep the whole of the top of the hill. They also have guns east; cannot you bring artillery fire to bear on north west guns? What reinforcements can you send to hold the hill tonight? We are badly in need of water. There are many killed and wounded

Alex Thorneycroft.

If you wish to really make a certainty of hill for tonight, you must send more infantry and attack enemy's guns.'

Coke added his view:

Spion Kop.
24th January 1900   3 p.m.

I have seen the above and have ordered the Scottish Rifles and King's Royal Rifles to reinforce. The Middlesex Regiment, Dorsetshire regiment, and Imp Light Infantry have also gone up, Bethune's mounted infantry (120 strong) also reinforce. We appear to be holding our own at present.

J. Talbot Coke
Major General.

Again, a layman cannot make a worthwhile comment on Coke's expression opinion, but this does seem to be a foolish opinion by a man who had not been near the top. His own report says, 'About 11.10 am, in consequence of the regrettable news about General Woodgate at your order I proceeded to the Kop myself...' but he never actually

reached the battleground. Further, Warren had no staff officers inform-
ing him of the success or otherwise of the supply system, particularly
water and medical requirements. There exists a note of a report that
Coke then took a nap. Coke, though, like Warren and Buller, was later
dissatisfied by the way reports treated him but was forbidden from
complaint.

While Warren struggled to decide what to do next, Lyttelton
answered his inappropriate cry for aid by sending men to help
Thorneycroft and groups to attack the so-called Twin Peaks; the idea
being to overlook Aloe Knoll one way and General Burger's camp the
other.

*Carrying on the northern edge, pass a British grave which the
guide says probably contains men who died in the morning, trying to
keep back the Boer counter-attack, before arriving at the Boer
Memorial, roughly in the middle of the northern rim, and on it are
recorded their dead. At this point reflect that from about 3.00 pm both
sides were stuck and it was the Boer artillery that was taking most
lives.*

Blomfield:

'So the battle went on all day. Rifle fire now and then
slackened a little, but the guns from N.W. and E. pounding
steadily away with horrible effect. The Boers were so close that

Some of the victors of Spion Kop.

their voices could be heard from among some rocks near at hand, but they showed no inclination to come to close quarters with our men. So close were the Boers that as we fixed bayonets many of them were hit, and Major Tidswell got a splinter in the neck from a bullet that struck his bayonet as it showed above the trench.

It was a terribly hot day, and the sufferings of the wounded lying all day in narrow trenches unable to move, and without water, were severe. Towards evening the order came that we were to retire, and those that had survived made the best of their way to the south end of the hill top to join the weary march back again across the Tugela.

Without sleep, without water, the men had throughout the day endured a most terrible fire from an enemy that was practically invisible. So heavy was the firing all day that carrying away of the wounded from the more forward and exposed trenches was impossible. Not until the welcome shades of night could their sufferings be alleviated, and in the darkness and confusion many were not found till morning.

Many were killed as they left the trenches, Sergeant Lightfoot, who had so pluckily helped to bring me in, among them. He had turned round in the trench and lifted his head to look out before starting, when a Boer marksman from the neighbouring rocks shot him through the head, and poor Lightfoot lay there dead.

After this a brisk fire was directed on the section of trench where we were, and my water-battle was shot off my chest as I lay on my back trying to make myself as small as possible. The Boers have an unsportsmanlike habit of continuing to fire at men they have wounded till the man lies absolutely still, when he is presumed to be dead. The slightest movement at once draws fire.

Private Bradley, of the Band, was in our trench shot through the chest and thigh, and when it grew dark I told him I would try and get up some stretcher bearers for the wounded who could not walk.

Unfortunately, I must have fainted soon after starting (my shoulder had been bleeding freely for the past nine hours), and when I came to again I must have headed in the wrong direction and got on the wrong side of the mountain, for at dawn next morning I found myself among a lot of Boers, who promptly made me a prisoner.'

The *Spion Kop Despatches* published in 1902 include Thorneycroft's later communication to Chief of Staff to Sir Charles Warren:

'The troops which marched up here last night are quite done up. Lancashire Fusiliers, Royal Lancaster Regt and Thorneycroft's Mounted Infantry. They have had no water and ammunition is running short. I consider that even with reinforcements which have arrived, that it is quite impossible to permanently hold this place so long as the enemy's guns can play on this hill. They have the long-range gun, three of shorter range, and one Maxim-Nordenfelt, which have swept the whole of the plateau since 8 a.m. I have been unable to ascertain the casualties, but they have been very heavy, especially in the regiments which came up last night. I request instructions as to what course I am to adopt. The enemy, at 6.30 pm, were firing heavily from both flanks with rifles, shell and a Nordenfelt, while a heavy rifle fire is kept up in front. It is all I can do to hold my own. If casualties   go on occurring at present rate I shall barely hold out the night. A large number of stretcher bearers should be sent up and also all water possible.The situation is critical.'

Reitz remained in his place until after 10 pm, listening to the cries of the wounded and to the talking of the British soldiers, before leaving with his Commandant, who had been there for sixteen hours. Again, Corporal Herbert's words in his letter are confirmed,'for the next sixteen hours our noses were buried into the ground except when firing.'

They felt beaten, and it is ironic that Brother Boer and Tommy Atkins were of one mind. Reitz says that his comrades expected to see the line broken in the morning and the British streaming through. But that was not how it turned out, and this time it was not due to Botha, although he turned up in nick of time and rallied the Burghers as so often.

Blomfield again,

'In the White Farm, some 3,000 yards to the north of the battlefield, the wounded were being dressed, and here Captain Elmslie (wounded in the shoulder and forearm, and with two cuts made by bullets that had furrowed the top of his head) joined me. He was very wroth at being made prisoner, as it appeared that General Louis Botha had given orders that he and some ten of our wounded men were to be taken to the British ambulance and not made prisoners. However, General Botha went away, and the next man in authority flatly and promptly disobeyed his General's orders. This meant 4½ months' captivity for these wounded.

The Boer treatment of the wounded was kind and considerate. Their standard of comfort is not high, but according to their lights the Boers on all occasions, so far as my observations went, did all they could for the wounded men. The sick prisoners-of-war in Waterfall was [sic] disgracefully treated, but for this a certain Dr. Veale in Pretoria was mainly responsible. The ordinary Boer seems to feel a good deal of sympathy for a wounded man, but not much for a sick man.'

By 7.00 pm it was going dark and neither side could influence the other so the Boers left and went down the hill where the lone figure of Botha attempted to stiffen them up. Unfortunately for him General Burger had taken his Commandos and their two pieces of artillery and gone. At 9 o'clock the direction on Warren's side again seemed to be poor for only then was a party put together to place the naval guns and improve the trenches. Coke was ordered back to HQ for a consultation but was never told that Thorneycroft was in charge. Indeed, he was never told of Warren's plans. When midnight came artillery, water, fresh troops and medical supplies were still not up the hill.

Then, at 4.00 am on the 24th a famous name appears in the story. Winston Churchill, – who besides being a war correspondent for the *Morning Post*, was serving as a Lieutenant in the South Africa Light Horse – without authority, rode out of camp and climbed to the top of the hill where the condition of the men, especially the wounded, left him so shocked that he went straight back to Warren's HQ, reported, and left immediately with news of the progress of the reinforcements for Thorneycroft. But this officer, who had done a magnificent job and had suffered all day with his men, decided to evacuate the hill and so led his men down, in his ignorance of Warren's plans.

Putland:
'After dark the firing eased and someone gave the order to retire, which was done during the night and being pitch dark and properly done up from the days events we was falling over boulders and rocks. The day's fight was done with rifle fire and artillery being out of range, they opened fire early morning and the shells burst among us so they ceased fire, whilst the Boers had big guns, Pompoms and rifles, and the pompom is an awful weapon (sic). During the time we were retiring they were also but they found out we had retired and came back and took up

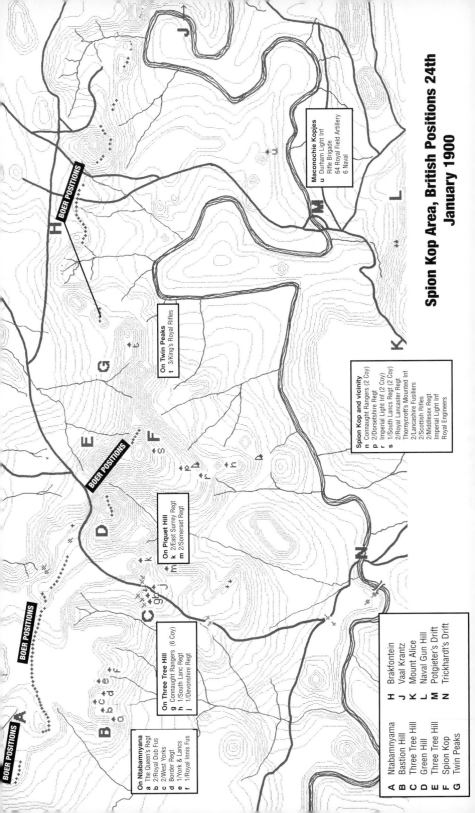

Spion Kop Area, British Positions 24th January 1900

BOER POSITIONS

BOER POSITIONS

BOER POSITIONS

BOER POSITIONS

Maconochie Kopies
u Durham Light Inf
Rifle Brigade
64 Royal Field Artillery
6 Naval

On Twin Peaks
t 3/King's Royal Rifles

Spion Kop and vicinity
n Connaught Rangers (2 Coy)
p 2/Dorsetshire Regt
r Imperial Light Inf (2 Coy)
s 1/South Lancs Regt (2 Coy)
2/Royal Lancaster Regt
Thornycroft's Mounted Inf
2/Lancashire Fusiliers
2/Scottish Rifles
2/Middlesex Regt
Imperial Light Inf
Royal Engineers

On Piquet Hill
k 2/East Surrey Regt
m 2/Somerset Regt

On Three Tree Hill
g Connaught Rangers (6 Coy)
h 1/South Lancs Regt
j 1/Devonshire Regt

On Ntabamnyama
a The Queen's Regt
b 2/Royal Dub Fus
c 2/West Yorks
d Border Regt
e 1/York & Lancs
f 1/Royal Innis Fus

A Ntabamnyama	H Brakfontein
B Bastion Hill	J Vaal Krantz
C Three Tree Hill	K Mount Alice
D Green Hill	L Naval Gun Hill
E Three Tree Hill	M Potgieter's Drift
F Spion Kop	N Trickhardt's Drift
G Twin Peaks	

their position again. This news we got from the escaped prisoners.'

There was further disarray at this point. Colonel Cooke, of the Scottish Rifles could not understand how Thorneycroft came to be in command; Colonel Crofton was his senior and also Lieutenant Colonel Hill (Middlesex Regiment) did not believe that Thorneycroft had been made a Brigadier, General Coke upholding him. Private Putland's record shows his regimental loyalty when he says, "we believe the retirement was ordered by Col. Thorneycroft, who had no right (sic). Colonel Hill was in command after General Woodgate fell but Colonel Hill thought the order came from Sir Charles Warren."

It was impossible to confirm or deny who was in command, impossible for private and colonel alike – the signaller was out of lamp-oil.

There are scattered Boer graves, and in same cases the trail-guide attempts an explanation of their meaning, though from the comment of everyone present it is difficult to find a meaning save that man is very much given to error and misinterpretation of information received. Carry on the sad round to the point where you began – where the Lancashire Fusiliers, the South Lancashires, the King's Own Royal Lancasters, Thorneycroft's and the Royal Engineers came on stage, many of them never to make an exit again.

At day-break the next day Reitz and his friends saw two men on the top waving their hats. They were Boers who had found the place empty, save for death and dread injury. The British a little later saw the same sight.

Winston Churchill was not the only famous twentieth century figure present at Spion Kop, for M. K. Ghandi was a humble stretcher-bearer, as he had been at the battle of Colenso, and on the day of truce that followed the action, he was involved in the sad caravan down the hill and on to Surgeon Treves at Spearman's.

Let Lieutenant Colonel Blomfield summarize,

'A few general remarks close this article. Much has been said about the enormous tactical advantage that would have been gained had Spion Kop been held. My own view is that the position was always absolutely untenable.

At the first glance, no doubt, it seemed a fine big mountain, from which the entire range north, north-west, and north-east of it could be commanded. From its summit you could see all the Boer positions away to the west towards Acton Homes, and to the eastward nearly to Vaal Krantz. But if the enemy on that long range of defences had guns (and we knew they had), the mountain slopes were obviously commanded themselves by a converging and enfolding fire from north-west and north-east, to say nothing of a direct fire from the north.

The top of the mountain was evidently small and very exposed to the north, to which it sloped downwards. Had our guns ever been got up they would not have remained in action ten minutes.

January 24th was not one of the days on which the Royal Artillery gained fresh laurels, and it was, indeed, fortunate for the gunners that they were unable to get guns to the top of Spion Kop.'

Blomfield then recounts a newspaper comment.

'In an interesting article, by Douglas Story, in the *Daily Mail*, occur these words:

"Our soldiers were, without exception, riflemen, and had not so much as the moral support of a bomb Maxim between them,. They had to stand like dumb driven sheep against a fire that raked them from the north, east and west. Occasionally from the south the British Batteries (sic) pitched a shell among the herd to signify that no mercy existed anywhere on earth for them.'"

Blomfield interjects,

'Whether the British Batteries did or did not at Spion Kop, as on other occasions, shell friend and foe with equal cheerfulness and impartiality I am not prepared to say, but from our own artillery we certainly received no assistance whatever on January 24th.'

He then continues with Douglas Story,

'Arrived at the summit, General Woodgate committed the same blunder Sir George Colley made at Majuba Hill 19 years before,' in not occupying the real crest, and thus obtaining the real command of fire.

This is true enough, in a sense, for there were certain pieces of dead ground in front of us which we could not properly command, but it is quite incorrect to say that we were not on the proper crest, speaking of the position as a whole.

The difficulty of the position lay in the formation of the hill top, on which there is very little flat ground, and to this difficulty was added the overwhelming one of the dense mist, to which reference has been made earlier.

No single correspondent, so far as I can learn, has ever, even

Lee-Metford .303 magazine rifle introduced into the British Army in 1888. Each round of ammunition had to be loaded into the box magazine indiviually – the magazine held ten rounds.

incidentally, referred to the morning mist and its disastrous consequences on the positions of the trenches we dug.

To turn to another point. In no accounts that I have been able to see, has any mention yet been made of the extremely skillful leadership of Lieutenant Colonel Thorneycroft of the column of some 1,600 men up the side of Spion Kop on the night preceding the battle.

To him is due all credit for the complete success of that most difficult and dangerous operation – a night march up the side of a rocky mountain that had not been reconnoitered. His march was a masterpiece in its way, yet Colonel Thorneycroft's part in it has never been mentioned.

The retirement from Spion Kop is a delicate question to deal with, but I am convinced that no other course was open to any sound commander than that adopted by Colonel Thorneycroft. By his decision to retire a repetition of the slaughter of the 24th on the next day was avoided.

There remains the question of the alleged Boer retreat from Spion Kop at the same time that we were withdrawing.

The Ladysmith garrison, watching with anxious eyes the battle raging all that long summer day, saw wagon after wagon moving from the Boer laagers and trekking to the north. So elated were the beleaguered force in Ladysmith that some of them with a few odds and ends of luxuries left, divided them among their friends as a sort of thank offering for the impending release! Perhaps the wish was father to the thought. Certainly the fighting Boers were not retreating at all. They were merely, with their usual acumen, sending away their impedimenta in good time to be ready for any emergency tomorrow.

As I was waiting to have my wound dressed, very early on the 25th, at the little farm just north of Spion Kop, parties of Boers were continually riding past the house up the hill to the battlefield. Moreover, the mountain battery taken from us before the Nicholson's Nek fiasco was also there going up to make all sure

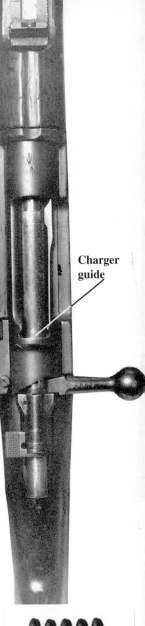

Charger guide

Left: The M1893 pattern Mauser rifle used to such good effect by the Boer farmers against the British Regular Army.

Above: A Boer farmer demonstrates the quick-feed method of loading using the charger clip inserted into the rifle's charger guide.

Right: A clip of five 7mm rounds in their brass charger which enabled the five-round magazine to be loaded at speed.

THE NATAL WITNESS

For Lieutenant the Hon. Neville Windsor Hill Trevor it was into the unknown, with two of the unknown.

for the Boers. I was told by a Free State doctor a few days later that so far from abandoning the position, Botha had ordered up 2,000 more Boers to be certain of holding on to Spion Kop at all costs.

It is quite true that General Schalk Burger (a most inferior soldier) retired in panic, but even he was shamed into coming back again after he had galloped a dozen miles to the north.

A curious story is told of the reason why the Boers refrained from firing on our force as we withdrew across the Tugela on the 25th. The tale relates that Louis Botha had received explicit orders that not a shot was to be fired at a fleeing man! This may be humanity, but it is not war, and my own theory is that the immunity of the British force, as it crossed the river, was due to the intervening hills and undulations of the lower ground, which covered the bridge from the Boer guns.

Nineteen officers of the Battalion had gone up the mountain side on the night of the 23rd; only seven remained unhurt. Five had been killed and seven wounded (all severely).

Of 800 men who had shared their officers' fortunes, hardly half came down again "fit for duty. "

It was some consolation to the survivors of that day to read later in dispatches that we had magnificently maintained the best traditions of the British army.'

The writer decided after a visit that mid-afternoon was a good time to leave, when the day was still in its pomp. The atmosphere of Spearman's the night before would not have worked, with its evening light and the Spearman family and the Zulu cowmen with their charges. There, those in the graves are guests who came for a while and became a part of the scene. Here, on Spioenkop there is no scene, not in that sense. For how many people ever came here from the world's creation until January 23rd 1900? The primitive natives who wandered by maybe, now and then; later on the Zulus – now and then – before the Voortrekkers in the late 1830s. Since then how many have been? Why would anyone come, except to best their enemies?

The Boers, decimated and in retreat themselves, had won the hill by

Wounded Boers from the Colenso front arriving in Pretoria.

THE NATAL WITNESS

A If the visitor turns around he will see some way in front of him the main British Memorial, so by looking at this picture and the one opposite (**C**) the whole length of the position is revealed. In front of the South Lancashire Memorial is that of Trooper C. Sleigh, 5th Lancers. Superimposed on his name is a further one, now weathered away.

B The South Lancashire Memorial.

C The main British Memorial, looking east. In this view the right face is the Kings Own Royal Lancaster Regiment, and on the left, Thorneycroft's Mounted Infantry. On the other faces the other units are listed. In front is Lieutenant Raymond Mallock of the Lancashire Fusiliers.

E Boer Grave: 'A Brave Burgher'.

D Main Boer Memorial.

default. We should leave the hill to the night, and the dew and rain to wet the remains, just as the sun and wind will dry them out again, on this useless corner of a foreign field.

The Commander in Chief, Lord Roberts, concluded his report on Spioenkop to the Secretary of State for War:

'The attempt to relieve Ladysmith, described in these despatches, was well devised, and I agree with Sir Redvers Buller in thinking that it ought to have succeeded. That it failed may, in some measure, be due to the difficulties of the ground and the commanding positions held by the the enemy - probably also to errors of judgement and want of administrative capacity on the part of Sir Charles Warren. But whatever faults Sir Charles Warren may have committed, the failure must also be ascribed to the disinclination of the officer in supreme command to assert his authority and see that what he thought best was done ,and

Lord Roberts of Kandahar, Commander-in-Chief in South Africa

also to the unwarrantable and needless assumption of responsibility by a subordinate officer.

The gratifying feature of these despatches is the admirable behaviour of the troops throughout the operations.'

As Corporal Herbert said, 'what was it all for? None of us know.'
Certainly the casualties in the whole episode did not know: not the 42 officers and 370 men who died, nor the 65 officers and 969 men who were wounded; not even the 2 officers and 285 men who went missing.

'What was it all for? None of us know.'

The Postscript that, by its anti-climactic understatement supports Corporal Herbert's remark is provided by the diary of the 2nd

Battalion The Lancashire Fusiliers, which concludes the matter:

'Jan 25th. Went into bivouac near Right's (sic) farm and rested. Did not get food until about 11 am.

Jan 26th. Whole force retired from its positions across the Tugela. Sat waiting in the rain from 10 p.m. till 4 am.

Jan 27th. Across Tugela River at 4.30 am. In evening moved towards Springfield, getting very wet. Bivouacked after dark.

Jan 28th. Camped near Hatting's farm in the morning.

Jan 29th. Paraded for Buller who complimented us.

Feb 3rd. 9th Brigade crossed at Potgieter's and bivouacked on bank.

Feb 5th. Took up position on Kopjes, while rest of Brigade and 73 guns made demonstration in front of Brakfontein positions: Clery's Division and Lyttelton's Brigade making the real attack on Vaal Krantz on the right, effecting lodgement on some Kopjes. Retirement of demonstrating troops was excellent, and though shelled considerably, suffered little loss. Went back to our bivouacs.

After the battle Boers, the victors of the hill, collect arms and equipment whilst British medical orderlies seek out and attend to the wounded.

Feb 6th. Started to recross the drift but eventually ordered to return to bivouac.

Feb 7th. Started for Zwart Kop about 4.30 am to support Clery's attack. Remained on hill all day, and bivouacked there for the night. Attacking force effected nothing.

Feb 8th. Returned to Spearman's Camp from Zwart Kop and en route sent to support Somerset Light Infantry on kopjes to north of river. Camped at Spearman's at 11 pm.

Feb 10th. Marched to Springfield Bridge in evening after covering retirement of X Brigade. Enemy did not attack.

Feb 12th. Reached Frere at 7.30 am with orders to garrison it, which, owing to our weakness, was an extremely difficult job.'

Imperial Light Infantry captured at Spion Kop en-route for Pretoria.

THE NATAL WITNESS

Chapter Four

HLANGWANE AND TUGELA HEIGHTS
17th-27th February 1900

General Buller was now in deep trouble, as were the Government. An Editorial on February 3rd 1900 in a provincial paper, the *Barnsley Chronicle*, summed the situation up:

'The King of France (sic), with twice ten thousand men,
Marched up the hill, and then marched down again.

We are irresistibly reminded of the words of the old political satire by recent events in South Africa. It is a singular parallel. We had the news last week – news which, after a long period of anxiety and suspense, sent a thrill of joyous gratitude through the heart of every Briton – of what was regarded as the first movement for the relief of Ladysmith, the taking of Spion Kop; but, alas! the cup of satisfaction is no sooner applied to our lips than it is dashed away again. Following closely upon it came the further intelligence that the British troops, after a most gallant defence in the face of a terrible fusillade upon them, had found the place untenable and had been obliged to abandon it, while, as

The Marquis of Salisbury
The Conservative
Prime Minister

Sir Henry Campbell-
Bannerman
Liberal Party

Winston Churchill
soldier, PoW, journalist;
later Member of Parliament

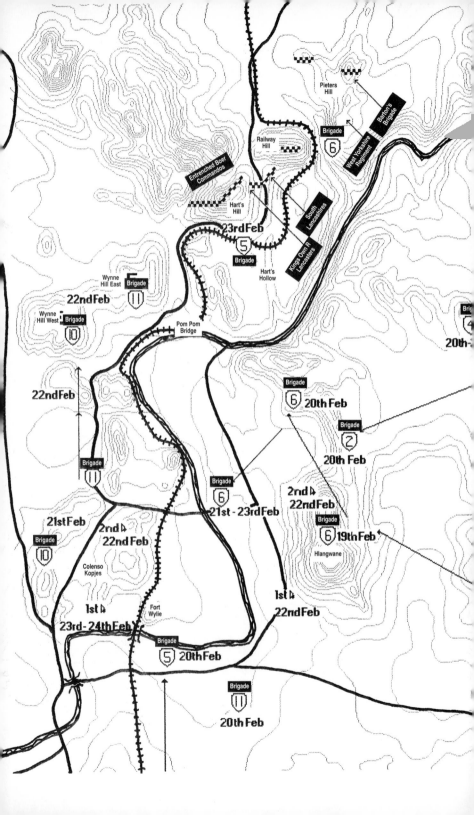

Pieters Hill

Railway Hill

Entrenched Boer Commandos

Hart's Hill

Barton's Brigade

West Yorkshire Regiment

Brigade **6**

23rd Feb

5
Brigade

South Lancashires

Kings Own R Lancasters

Hart's Hollow

Wynne Hill East Brigade **11**

22nd Feb

Wynne Hill West Brigade **10**

Pom Pom Bridge

Brigade **4**

20th

22ndFeb

Brigade **6** **20th Feb**

Brigade **2**

20th Feb

Brigade **11**

2nd
22nd Feb

Brigade **6**
21st - 23rd Feb

Brigade **6** **19th Feb**

21stFeb

Brigade **10**

2nd
22nd Feb

Hlangwane

Colenso Kopjes

1st
23rd - 24th Feb

Fort Wylie

Brigade **5** **20th Feb**

1st
22nd Feb

Brigade **11**

20th Feb

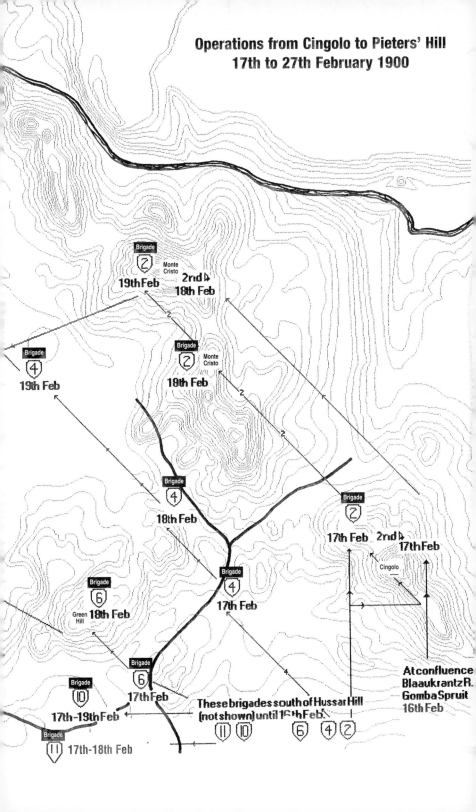

**Operations from Cingolo to Pieters' Hill
17th to 27th February 1900**

Brigade **2** Monte Cristo **19th Feb**   **2nd △ 18th Feb**

Brigade **4** **19th Feb**

Brigade **2** Monte Cristo **18th Feb**

Brigade **4** **18th Feb**

Brigade **2**

17th Feb   2nd △   **17th Feb**

Cingolo

Brigade **4** **17th Feb**

Brigade **6** Green Hill **18th Feb**

Brigade **6** **17th Feb**

Brigade **10** **17th-19th Feb**

At confluence Blaaukrantz R. Gomba Spruit 16th Feb

These brigades south of Hussar Hill (not shown) until 16th Feb   **11** **10**   **6** **4** **2**

Brigade **11** **17th-18th Feb**

a practical admission of the failure of the whole movement, General Buller had been obliged to retreat once more across the Tugela, in defiance of his own declaration that "there is to be no turning back"... It is an awful admission of failure. We do not blame the Generals.'

But they did, and, as far as the dangers were understood, they had to. The Government, however, bore the greater blame for the editorial continued:

'How is it that we ever came to be in this position of humiliation and danger? The time has arrived when that question can be asked. Parliament met on Tuesday, and the question was asked – by Lord Kimberley in the Lords and by Sir H. Campbell Bannerman in the Commons. But we are sorry to say that the nation, which has been so patiently watching and wanting to know what the Government are going to do to redeem the position which their lack of foresight and their incompetence have produced, can derive little satisfaction from the Ministerial oratory.'

This was on Saturday, February 3rd, and the next response was on the 5th – the aborted operation at Vaal Krantz.

Buller, under the weight of his back-breaking problems, could only keep trying. He decided it was impossible to force the Boer lines directly and returned to an idea that many thought had always been obvious. The Boers, meanwhile, had already realized that the route now selected by Buller was the logical key to the enemy taking their positions. They therefore improved the fortifications from Hlangwane to Green Hill, Monte Cristo and Cingolo, which was, effectively, the end of their line. Further, they constructed temporary bridges north of Hlangwane, under Naval Hill. So it was that on 7th February Buller concluded that he needed to take these hills in order to crack the Boer defences. The main body of the army was situated at Chieveley railway station where Buller's HQ was; his extreme left was at Springfield where Lieutenant Colonel Burn-Murdoch of the Royal Dragoons had the 1st Cavalry Brigade, 'A' battery Royal Horse Artillery; two Naval 12-pdrs; the 1st York and Lancaster, and the Imperial Light Infantry (said to be 106 officers and 2680 other ranks in total); and the right flank down at Greytown, where there were men of Bethune's Mounted Infantry, Natal Police, Umvoti Mounted Rifles and the Natal Field Artillery with two 7-pdr Field Guns – all 460 men under the command of Lieutenant Colonel E. C. Bethune.

It would be sensible to join a party and use an official Guide for this area as a matter of security, as while the distances are small and the population sparse, it could be very exposed. In any case, the injunction 'ask the locals,' very much applies – and then pay attention to advice received. Large parts of the area that will now be covered are privately owned, and also just as there is a different and more violent atmosphere among people than was known years ago in the UK, there is in South Africa. On the other hand, with South African tourism fast becoming more practicable for ordinary folk from Europe and the increased opportunities for income that this implies, it is unthinkable that the authorities and entrepreneurs will not work together to improve public access to the sites.

The start is back at Clouston, effectively in the midst of the British base. Again the camp is hard to visualize because, apart from the occasional road and rail traffic, it is the wind and insects that make the greatest noise. On a sunny day all is peace and calm. If one faces Colenso again and then looks to the right beyond the railway the clumps of trees and odd buildings make a near horizon so that Hussar Hill cannot easily be identified, but on February 12th Lord Dundonald temporarily took control of that rise allowing Buller to study the ground in person before withdrawing the men. If one looks at the distant cooling-towers and then to the half-right, Hlangwane is clearly visible with Cingolo leading back from it running south-east to north-west to Monte Cristo. In viewing events the tourer shares with the newsmen of the day the problem that, unlike Colenso, or even Spion Kop, the topography here and the nature of the fighting makes it less spectacular. The work was efficiently done but, as one journalist said, 'more than half invisible'

The main army at Chieveley was as follows:

Headquarters Staff with the Naval Brigade of 30 officers and 305 other ranks, under Captain E. P. Jones, RN, serving the following
One 6″ gun,
Three 4.7" guns - and three more which arrived after a day or two.
Ten 12 pounder, 12 cwt guns.
19th battery R.F.A.
61st Howitzer battery R.F.A.
Two 5" guns, with two more later on.
No. 4 Mountain battery R.F.A.
Ammunition column.
Telegraph detachment R.E.
A. Pontoon Troop R.E.
Balloon Section R.E.

2nd Mounted Brigade (Colonel the Earl of Dundonald.):
   Composite Regiment of Mounted Cavalry.
   South African Light Horse.
   Thorneycroft's Mounted Infantry

IInd Infantry Division (Major-General the Hon. N. G. Lyttelton.):
   Divisional Troops:
   1 troop 13th Hussars.
   7th battery   R.F.A.}
   63rd battery R.F.A.}   Brigade Division R.F.A.
   64th battery R.F.A.}
   Ammunition Column.
   17th Company R.E.

2 Brigade (Major-General H. J. T. Hildyard):
   2nd Battalion "Queen's" Regiment.
   2nd Battalion Devonshire Regiment.
   2nd Battalion West Yorkshire Regiment.
   2nd Battalion East Surrey Regiment.

4 Brigade (Colonel C. H. B. Norcott, vice Major-General
the Hon N. G.. Lyttelton):
   2nd Battalion Scottish Rifles.
   3rd Battalion King's Royal Rifle Corps.
   1st Battalion Durham Light Infantry.
   1st Battalion Rifle Brigade.

Vth Infantry Division (under Lieutenant-General Sir C. Warren)

Divisional Troops:
   1 troop Royal Dragoons.
   Colonial Scouts.
   28th battery R.F.A.}
   73rd battery R.F.A. } Brigade Division R.F.A.
   78th battery R.F.A }
   Ammunition Column.
   37th company R.E.

10 Brigade (under Major-General J. Talbot Coke)
   2nd Battalion Somerset Light Infantry.
   2nd Battalion Dorset Regiment.
   2nd Battalion Middlesex Regiment.

11 Brigade (under Major-General A. S. Wynne)
   2nd Battalion King's Own (Royal Lancaster) Regiment.
   1st Battalion South Lancashire Regiment.
   Rifle Reserve battalion.

6 Brigade - temporarily attached to Vth Division - (under Major-General G. Barton)

2nd Battalion Royal Fusiliers.
2nd Battalion Royal Scots Fusiliers.
1st Battalion Royal Welsh Fusiliers.
2nd Battalion Royal Irish Fusiliers.

5 Brigade - unattached - (under Major-General A. F. Hart)

1st Battalion Royal Inniskilling Fusiliers.
1st Battalion Border Regiment.
1st Battalion Connaught Rangers.
2nd Battalion Royal Dublin Fusiliers.

* The York and Lancs as well as the Lancashire Fusiliers had been detached from the 11th brigade.

There were available in all 24507 men with 831 officers. They had 42 Field Guns, six Howitzers, six mountain guns, one 6″ gun, two 5″ guns, 22 machine guns and the naval guns.

Buller informed White at Ladysmith that he intended to attempt to take Hlangwane, Green Hill,

Captain P Scott, CB, RN who modified 45 pounder (4.7 inch) and 12 pounder ships' guns to serve as land artillery.

British 12 pounder field gun.

Cingolo and Monte Cristo, moving eastwards far enough to clear the nearer bank of the river. General Buller benefited from the report on the whole of the enemy position, prepared by Lieutenant Colonel A. E. Sandbach, paying attention to the artillery pieces in place. He then

Dispositions for attack on Hlangwana

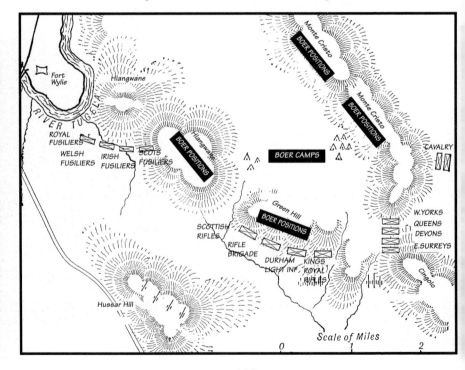

gave orders to his men verbally, as he had little means of describing in written notes the features of the area, which was often without landmarks. The weather at that time was very hot and others since have remarked on the stultifying effect of Natal's midsummer sun. Water was short. Buller claimed that the delay that he now imposed on the advance was to rest the men, but even at rest they were constantly under shell fire. Water being short still did not stop General Warren having a bath in a mackintosh-lined shell-hole, which provided a diversion for the men.

On 14th February Hussar Hill was occupied and the Boers' 94 pounder gun at Fort Wylie silenced by the British artillery on Gun Hill. Further guns could now be posted on Hussar Hill so as to shell the enemy between Hlangwane and Green Hill and the 15th was devoted to an artillery barrage before making a reconnaissance of Cingolo on the 16th.

On the 17th Lyttelton was instructed to cross the Gomba river, running east to west, south of Cingolo hill, and the IInd Division, which had spent the night opposite that hill, was to swing leftwards and attack Green Hill. At dawn the 4.7s opened up.

West Yorks attacking at Monte Cristo.

Naval Brigade with a 4.7″ on Hlangwane.

Lieutenant Colonel F W Kitchener, younger brother of Lord Kitchener
'Give me the guns...'

Hildyard with the 2nd Brigade moved onto Cingolo at 6.30 am using the 2nd West Yorks in the lead, followed by the 2nd Devons, 2nd Queens and 2nd East Surreys. Meanwhile, Dundonald's 2nd Mounted Brigade and Composite Regiment climbed up the opposite side and were on top by 1.00 pm. The hill was captured by 4.00 pm.

From 'Ladysmith 4th March 1900', Lieutenant Francis of the West Yorks wrote of this episode,

'...the brigade was ordered to advance... and took Redpatch Hill (in front of Monte Cristo). The Queens forced their way up Zingolo (sic), but the gunners said they could never be got up there – whereupon the Colonel said, "Give me the guns and I will get them up."'

A battery was brought to Red Patch Hill and the West Yorks, along with the Devons, worked through the night so that the artillery was in place by morning, bearing on Monte Cristo.

On the 18th at dawn they began firing and at 6.40 2 Brigade advanced with the West Yorks on the left and the Queen's on the right, followed by the East Surreys and the Devons. They faced fire from Hlangwane, Green Hill, Pieters and Monte itself. A position was claimed by the leading regiments on the southernmost point of Monte Cristo, a ridge running roughly NNW/SSE.

Supported by artillery, Hildyard and Dundonald between them cleared the hill, and as the Boers made off Buller refused to allow the advance to continue, preferring to make a road up the nek so as to bring up heavy guns. Meanwhile, 10th Brigade sent men to support 6th Brigade so that on the 18th, a Sunday, Green Hill was taken, leaving Hart at Chieveley and Wynne at Hussar Hill. Francis again,

'We were treated for the first time with a panoramic view of
the Boers in full retreat until night fell and the pursuit stopped.'

Barton's Brigade captured Hlangwane on the 19th and now heavy artillery could be moved there to shell Pieters Hill across the Tugela. Although the Boers started to move northwards, apparently disorganized, Botha once more re-positioned his men, again showing himself to be the most able leader in this theatre, if not of the whole war; and by 7 am on the 20th there were no Boers on the south bank of the Tugela. Sir Redvers Buller could now climb Monte Cristo in the afternoon and give a close consideration to the whole area.

You might now wish to give close consideration to your hunger, and, if so, the Battlefield Hotel is on the main road in Colenso. They do a very good fish (King Klip) and chips, though we found the service slow, and we had been told that there is a good number of photographs on the walls. There is, and some of them less common, but take a torch. The main bar has low lights, low both in intensity and height; which might be all right for a private drink and an intimate conversation, but is no good for studying historical pictures. So have your torch in the car!

Buller decided that a pontoon bridge between Fort Wylie and the falls was the best method of attack, as to go downstream towards the river's confluence with the Klip would bring even greater problems, so at 5.30 am on February 21st, with artillery in place, Major-General Barton covered the river at the foot of Hlangwane, while the Royal Engineers constructed the bridge. This rejected the advantage of having the Boer position in enfilade from Monte Cristo, and seemed to put him back in the situation that he had been so often before, that of being overlooked by a strong defensive position, in this instance the sweep of hills ending with Pieters' in the east.

Even though the new route eschewed Monte Cristo's value, the British artillery offered those crossing the river great protection, and one must not forget the apparent disorganization of the Boers mentioned earlier. That this was something of an illusion is shown by the fact that, once the enemy had seen Buller's intention, they immediately strengthened their new position along that same defensive line of what would become known as Pieters, Railway, Harts and Wynne Hills.

Buller paused at Monte Cristo and you may have done at the Battlefield Hotel, but now follow the 'Tugela Ferryman' across the river yet again. An overview of the area can be had from the Colenso-Pieters-Ladysmith Road. After crossing the Bulwer Bridge turn right so that the route brings you round the back of Fort Wylie. As the road sweeps upwards the railway runs on an embankment to the right before disappearing from view, and eventually the road climbs up onto a broad upland with Pieters station now on the right. Here, turning

British crossing the Tugela.

Memorials in front of Wynne Hill. Just along the road, to the right, is the Somerset's Memorial, and, beyond that, the lane leading to Pom Pom Bridge.

round and going back steadily to the brow you can see over the railway, now to the left and below, the course of the Tugela. It meanders through the hills in its ravine with a waterfall and rapids interrupting its flow, and if, in relation to the Rhine, or even the Thames, it looks small, look again. Clearly it may not be a big river by European standards, much less American, but it is a very self-willed stream, and even when it is behaving well the bottom of the gully is still overlooked by the hills.

Beware, however, of traffic. Here is an instance where the road is good if not particularly wide, but the traffic fast. Parking places are in short supply so it would be better to have company and try to

131

IN MEMORY OF BRITISH SOLDIERS
KILLED IN THE OPERATIONS NEAR
THE ONDERBROEK SPRUIT BETWEEN
THE 22ND AND 24TH FEBRUARY, 1900
WHO REST BENEATH THIS STONE

ROYAL FIELD ARTILLERY
DRIVER   J. BOSHER   61 BATTERY
GUNNER   T. HUMPHREY   61 BATTERY
GUNNER   T. SUMMER   73 BATTERY
GUNNER   G. J. TUCKER   73 BATTERY

QUEENS ROYAL REGIMENT WEST SURREY
LIEUT.   B. H. HASTIE
PRIVATE LIZIMORE

KINGS OWN ROYAL REGIMENT LANCASTER
LIEUT.   R. C. C. COE
PRIVATE B. MURRAY
PRIVATE J. ROBERTS

ROYAL WELCH FUSILIERS
LIEUT.   F. A. STEBBINGS
PRIVATE G. COX
PRIVATE E. EVANS
PRIVATE W. JEPHCOTE
PRIVATE S. PIKE
PRIVATE W. WILLIAMS

ROYAL INNISKILLING FUSILIERS
L.CORPORAL R. WATSON
PRIVATE P. M. GRATH

EAST SURREY REGIMENT
PRIVATE PRYOR

DORSET REGIMENT
PRIVATE J. NEAL
PRIVATE H. LUGG

SOUTH LANCASHIRE REGIMENT
PRIVATE T. S. MARSCROFT
PRIVATE H. WALMESLEY

MIDDLESEX REGIMENT
SGT.   CHAMBERLAIN
PRIVATE GILLEN
PRIVATE W. McMANUS
PRIVATE E. SMITH

ROYAL DUBLIN FUSILIERS
PRIVATE H. MARTIN

KINGS ROYAL RIFLE CORPS
CORAL P. JONES
PRIVATE A. ANDREWS
SEVERAL UNKNOWN BRAVE SOLDIERS
They shall remember in far countries

CONSECRATED BY THE RIGHT REVEREND
1983

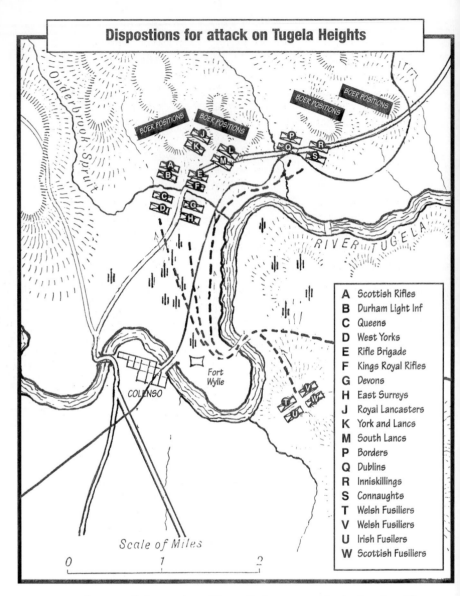

Dispostions for attack on Tugela Heights

BOER POSITIONS

A	Scottish Rifles
B	Durham Light Inf
C	Queens
D	West Yorks
E	Rifle Brigade
F	Kings Royal Rifles
G	Devons
H	East Surreys
J	Royal Lancasters
K	York and Lancs
M	South Lancs
P	Borders
Q	Dublins
R	Inniskillings
S	Connaughts
T	Welsh Fusiliers
V	Welsh Fusiliers
U	Irish Fusiliers
W	Scottish Fusiliers

RIVER TUGELA

Fort Wylie

COLENSO

Onderbrook Spruit

Scale of Miles

0   1   2

get the car off the road, walking a little way to take in the view. The drawing from Harts' Hill in The Official History of the War in South Africa gives a good impression.

When the Somersets were thrown in as the spearhead they took a beating before establishing themselves. Look first of all at a group of memorials on the left beside the road. They commemorate the *regiments which were involved in the Onderbroek confrontation, before the Somersets' memorial on the right. Increasingly, you can see that all around are places to hide, but anyone wishing to move is exposed from more than one direction. Wynne Hill, in front, above and to the left was thought to be the easiest spot to make progress. The National Monuments Council's plaque here reads, 'In his fourth and final attempt to raise the siege of Ladysmith Gen. Buller, in command of about 30,000 British troops, launched an attack on the Boer positions south of the Tugela River. On 21 February he forced the crossing of the river and attacked Gen. Louis Botha's skillfully prepared positions in the hills on the north side, manned by about 6000 Burghers. After unsuccessful attempts on Grobbelaar's Kloof, Wynne Hill and Hart's Hill, the British forces broke through the Boer line between Hart's Hill, Railway Hill and at Pieter's Hill on 27 February.'*

At the western end of this line was high, rough ground unsuitable to the attackers, so the best approach was now thought to be to get control of the lower hills at the rear of Fort Wylie and then launch an attack on the first large kop northwards. The Somersets and others of Coke's 10 Brigade, mauled as they had been when they first crossed, were now strong enough to hold the left flank while Wynne's South Lancashires and Royal Lancasters and composite Rifle Brigade attempted to take the higher ground in front, now known as Wynne Hill. According to *The Times History of the War in South Africa* it is approximately a mile wide by some 300 yards to half a

Major-General A S Wynne, CB 11 Brigade

mile across and was both heavily defended and overlooked all round. Wynne was quickly wounded and temporarily replaced by Colonel Crofton who had performed the same task on Spion Kop. The battle swept back and forth across the summit with the bayonet in use as well as the rifle until they gradually won enough control for the advance to continue along the railway line behind them. However, when Day Two after the crossing dawned, 23rd February, the next stage had to be faced and that involved going into the open.

We met Private Bryant of the 1st Inniskillings at the Battle of Colenso in December and, after nearly being drowned in the Tugela up near Spearmans, he was back again there on 22nd February.

'We arrived at Colenso at 6am after marching about nine miles or so. We passed by the Railway Bridge which was totally wrecked, it having been blown up by the Boers, and we rejoined

Buller's main force once more. The Boers thinking that they would never be put out of Colenso, had brought their beds, etc., down with them and had them in bomb proof shelters. We bivouacked for the day, which was a very hot one, and some of the men of the Brigade went exploring and came across boxes of explosive bullets which the Boers had been using. The Battle for the Relief of Ladysmith had to shift to another place, and we lay down near one of our Howitzer batteries; we had a few casualties whilst shifting our position. The Imperial Light Infantry (a Colonial Corps) were (*sic*) attached to our Brigade, in place of the Border Regiment who were elsewhere. A few shells kept coming pretty near to us from the Boers' guns, as they were trying to find the range of our Howitzer Battery, and succeeded after we left. The Irish Brigade received orders to go into action during the afternoon. The Inniskillings were to Form the Firing Line; the Dublins and Connaughts the support, and the ILI were the reserves.'

The railway crossed over the Langverwacht stream by a bridge and because the river was running fast and its banks muddy it was lunch-time before they made progress over it. The enemy was entrenched on what was to be called Harts or Inniskilling Hill as well as being massed up the Langverwacht valley. The Irishmen were completely exposed as they crossed. A pompom was trained on the latticed sides and heavy

Opposite below: **Pom Pom Bridge with Tugela River in background as viewed by Boers on 23 February 1900.** (Province of Kwazulu-Natal Museum Service.)
Above **Royal Engineers later shielded the sides with sandbags** (Steve A Watt)
Below **Pom Pom Bridge in the 1980s, the railway having been re-routed earlier this century. The whole embankment is now considerably overgrown.** (Steve A Watt)

casualties were taken. With his usual clever and matter-of-fact observation Tommy Atkins named the feature Pom Pom Bridge and the name stuck. Somehow we, the bystanders, seem to have been here before, as the amazingly cool bravery of the men prepared to do just as they were told on Spion Kop is recalled on the one hand, and Hart's preparedness to throw lives away in the Loop at Colenso is remembered on the other.

From the Somerset Memorial there is a good view across the road to Wynnes, while behind you is the railway embankment which was thrown up when the line was re-routed earlier this century.

Near the Memorial a farm-track goes down through an arch in the embankment. A vast puddle is to be found under the bridge, followed by an impressive collection of stones and rocks of all sizes, hidden in the long grass between the wheel-ruts. Farm gates have to be dealt with and the visitor is urged to close them behind him. Here is where the Langverwacht Spruit empties into the Tugela River although one would not know without close examination. Leaving the car and pushing a few yards to the right is the tumble down the bank to the edge of the spruit – in the writer's case, at the expense of lashed legs, and having permitted right of way to a huge and dramatically marked spider in an overhanging bush. It is a pretty, sylvan spot in the sunshine with profuse growth, and the pools of the spruit almost idle when the writer saw them. The piers of Pom Pom Bridge are now blurred and softened by the passage of time, so that they look as if they belong there although they have had no purpose for years. There is now no suggestion of the desperate day in February 1900 when the structure got its name. Indeed, if you climb up onto the embankment, Africa has asserted herself so thoroughly that the man-made shape of the railway line is hidden.

There are paths around Hart's Hill, though it must be stressed that local help is called for unless, possibly even if, you are a member of a party. The area is almost as remote today as it was at the time of the battle and is every bit as wild and tangled. It is well worth the trouble taken, and one is staggered by the difficulty that Hart and his long-suffering men faced with determined and well-equipped enemies on every height.

The prose with which Private Bryant confided in his diary illustrates that cool, almost mechanical dedication to duty.

'We had to cross over a small Railway Bridge, whilst on our march to the place of our operations, and we were open to a very murderous fire from the Boer mausers, as they had the Range off to a T (*sic*) and we had to run the gauntlet, but did not have many casualties for all that.'

The ridge of what became known as Hart's or Inniskilling Hill was, as usual, lined by the Boer defences, and late in the day Major-General Fitzroy Hart sent his Irish Brigade up the steep hill in columns, watched by General Lyttelton. At that time the hill was bare, though today it is well covered by trees, and observers, including Winston Churchill, remarked on the ferocity and volume of the Boer fusillade (*London to Ladysmith*, From the Hospital Ship *Maine* 5th March 1900). It was tea-time when the climb started and *The Times History* tells us that Hart had his bugler repeatedly sound the 'double' and the 'charge' to urge the men up. Again Hart displayed his capacity for ordering men to do things at all costs, and the costs now were expensive with Lieutenant Colonel Thackeray, who had been rebuked by Hart at Colenso for being in the right place when Hart was not, was now killed. The artillery pounded the trench-line but the

Lieutenant-Colonel Thackeray Inniskilling Fusiliers

The Inniskilling Fusiliers tried to complete the job at Hart's Hill.

Boers – more than a match for the Regulars of the British Army. Note the three standing are posing with clips placed in the charger guides of their Mauser rifles.

Boers continued to stand up to fire down on the attackers with no respect for rank or family; half the total force fell including two colonels, three majors, and twenty other officers. The Inniskilling Fusiliers just had not got the width or the numbers of men to complete the job and the Connaughts and the Dublins could not effect a greater change although they threw themselves in with their comrades.

Overnight the troops left the hill and although they were joined by two battalions of fresh troops the next morning, the 24th, no further progress could be made.

Private Bryant again,

'We had to drive the Boers from three positions; the last being called Pieters or Railway Hill, from which this battle takes its name. The Boers evacuated the first position, and our chaps charged the second position and drove the Boers from it. The last position was a very precipitous and stony hill, but the Regt under

Lieut Col T. M. G. Thackeray made a dash for it at once, but such a murderous fire was opened on them, that they could not stand it and were repulsed with heavy loss. Col: Thackeray was one of the men who fell mortally wounded in that desperate charge. Not to be denied, the men under command of Major Saunders, with a company of the Dublins and Connaughts, again made a rush for the position, but were again repulsed with frightful loss, being unable to stand long under such a fire as was brought to bear on them. Darkness having then set in, the Battalion retired back to the position they had won and held it for the night. The Boers were sniping all night long. It was impossible to go near the place, let alone carry a man away on a stretcher.

Some of our wounded men, who were lying quite near the Boer position, told us that they suffered from want of water, and that the Boers robbed our dead, as usual.'

To find Thackeray's marker another right turn, this time before Pieters Station, will lead us back and down Hart's Hill, across the quarry railway to a group of memorials. Again, guidance would be advisable.

Lieutenant Francis of the West Yorks, meanwhile, was having his

Graves of the Royal Inniskilling and the Dublin Fusilliers at the foot of Hart's Hill after the ill-fated attack by the Irish Brigade. The Natal Witness

own adventures.

'On the evening of the 23rd. the Regiment moved on further while I had gone back for rations for them. I went back to find where they were and found a road. The C.O. said he would leave a sentry on the road to stop us as we passed the place to turn off

The need for a pontoon bridge is illustrated here by this photograph of the vulnerability of ox carts crossing a drift. The Natal Witness

for the Regiment. I went back and brought up the oxen and went strolling along the road with the wagon. After going a very long way I came under a hill, and not recognizing it, I went up it a little shouting, "Are the West Yorks there!" I found (later) that we had gone right up to the Boer main position and I had been shouting up the hill which Hart afterwards attacked and failed to take.'

Private Bryant's diary tells us that on the 24th his regiment was retired, and they rested near to the river. A Muster Roll Call, he says, revealed that they had lost 69 men killed and about 175 wounded including their colonel and second in command.

"No further fighting took place today as it was raining all day.'

Hart's Hill was yet another setback but another reconnaissance by Lieutenant Colonel Sandbach showed that the Tugela could be crossed further downstream, Buller decided to attack the most easterly Kop (Pieters Hill), and move westward across Railway Hill to Hart's or Inniskilling Hill.

On Sunday the 25th a proper truce began so that the wounded could be brought down from Wynne's and Harts where some had lain for two or even three nights without rations or drinks, so until sundown Boers and British were in physical contact and for many British soldiers it was the first time they had seen one of the enemy. Many strange interviews were had, though the initial moments of individual personal contact must have been very dangerous. One account told of a magnificent specimen of manhood who appeared from a trench, one Commandant Pristorius, a lawyer in peace-time but a bearded soldier now, along with an array of old men, young men and boys. There were bearded figures in old suits and bandoliers along with young boys with whispy down on their juvenile jaws; all of them, once the ice was broken, accepting gifts of tobacco. For a time the only work at the front was humanitarian, before the killing began again, which allowed Buller, as he legitimately could, to re-arrange his forces. While holding the position on Wynne's the artillery was moved back across the river to be positioned opposite Hart's Hill and after dark the pontoon bridge was dismantled and moved downstream, while Monday was spent in finishing the plan and instructing the senior officers.

At this time the Boers were beginning to lose their resolve. The magnificence of their defence had sapped them and the discipline of their adversary and his seemingly endless supplies were wearing them done.

The 27th was the anniversary of Majuba Hill in 1881 and news was to hand and passed round that General Cronje had surrendered to Lord Roberts at Paardeburg. By mid-morning the pontoon bridge was reassembled and Lieutenant Colonel L. W. Parsons' guns were providing the creeping curtain of shell-fire in front of the toiling infantry. After crossing, Major-General G. Barton directed his men downstream almost on the riverbank until they were directly below **The re-routed railway perpetuates the sad 23 February 1900 by this wayside halt.**

Pieters, and the Boers were mainly prevented from seeing what was going on by the artillery barrage. Part of the steep climb could be accomplished under cover but as they came onto the tableland below the actual hill they were in full view of the burghers. With the Irish on the left and the Scots on the right they charged into the teeth of the enormous Boer fusillade and though they secured themselves on the left and centre, on the right the Scots were hard pressed. They then, after three hours fighting, became bogged down under the defenders' guns.

5 Brigade under Walter Kitchener, brother of Lord Kitchener, also moved down the river as far as the end of Railway Hill, where he sent some of his own West Yorks up the ravine as discretely as possible, with Lancashire men making up the centre and left. They forced their way up the steep hill right to the very top, where, as so often before, the Boers had fallen back to a secondary and heavily manned position; but this time the defenders were unable to stop the charge and were overcome. They did so well that on the left flank men of the King's Own swarmed across to Hart's also and began to strafe the Boer trench there. Here they were assisting Norcott's brigade and some of Hildyard's.

The Inniskillings were still in the thick of it and Private Bryant had yet more to tell his diary:

'Our regiment went into action again... Captain Gibton took over the command of the Btn as we only have 4 officers left and he is the Senior.[*sic*] [Captain W. L. P. Gibton who, after entering Ladysmith, died of enteric fever.] General Buller having shifted his guns to another position turned the lot on the Boers' position, which they effectively shelled with Lyddite and shrapnell [*sic*] all the morning and afternoon, so that the Boers dare not lift up their heads, knowing that they would get a warm reception. We had about 94 guns playing on the Boer trenches and they were firing Salvoes (volleys) and the noise they made would make your head split. About 3 pm, our troops charged the Boers' position in overwhelming numbers, and the Boers ran for their lives out of their trenches, a lot of them showing the white flag and holding up their hands, but the chaps were that mad they took no notice of them at the start, and down they went. The Boers must have lost pretty heavy today; our losses being 1500. We had 4 casualties in our regiment today.'

But it was the South Lancashires who took the bayonet to the enemy and separated Railway Hill from Hart's Hill. *The South Lancashire*

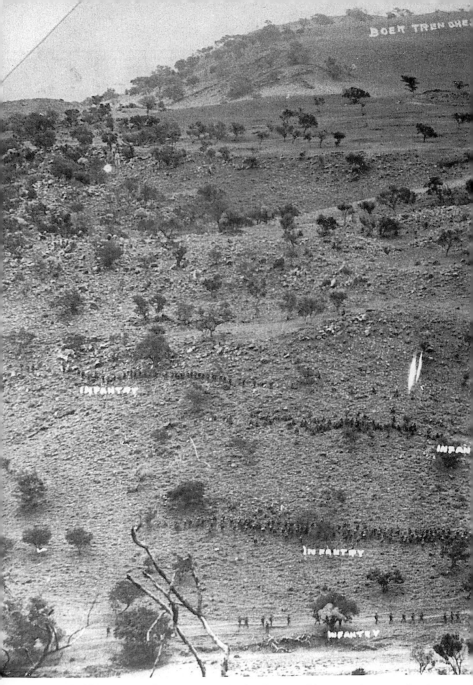

British troops advance to attack the Boer positions on the summit of Hart's Hill 27 February 1900.

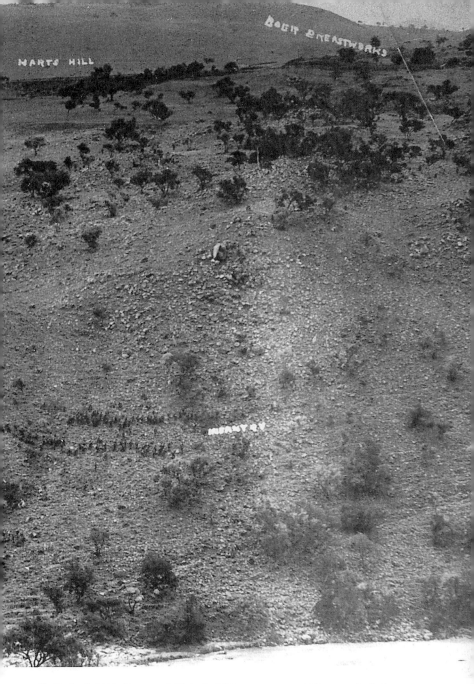

To their right Railway and Pieter's Hills were successfully assaulted that day to break the Tugela Line. Steve A. Watt

Hart's Hill, same view in the 1980s. Note quarry, now closed, near the left shoulder of the hill. The River Tugela is visible in the foreground. Steve A. Watt

Regiment The Prince of Wales's Volunteers tells us that the Lancashire Brigade climbed Railway Hill in extended lines and when 300 yards from Boer trenches prepared to rush in. Bayonets were fixed and Colonel McCarthy O'Leary cried, 'Remember, men, the eyes of Lancashire are watching you.' T. Neligan, who was present and is yet another of 1900's other ranks who could put pen to paper, wrote,

'At his words the whole regiment rose like one man, and the black slope fairly twinkled with the glitter of bayonets as they flashed in the sun. Like a wall of rock the gallant 40th closed upon their foe, and the best disciplined troops in the world could not have withstood that irresistable rush.'

Colonel McCarthy O'Leary was killed as his men swarmed up and into the trenches.

We met Lance Corporal C. Bradley of 'H' Company earlier on those awful wet days as they foot-slogged up to Springfield, and when he had crossed the pontoon bridge back on 21st February he too could comment afterwards.

'Our colonel, seeing we were getting no advantage in this way gave the order to fix bayonets and prepare to charge and immediately received a bullet wound but he got in front and shouted "charge" and again he received two more wounds and dropped. I think these were his last words as he expired soon after, but his last command was carried out to the letter as we took the trenches and captured I should say at least 50 or 60 prisoners.'

Colonel McCarthy O'Leary was buried near the spot, the original Grave Record saying ' about 50 yards S. of Cutting S. of Pieters Station', and he lies with four of his comrades. If his end sounds dramatic it has to be said that he made a great impression on his men. The dairy of Colour-Sergeant H. Cleaver in the keeping of the museum of The Queen's Lancashire Regiment contains this poem,

Colonel McCarthy O'Leary, 1st Battalion South Lancashire Regiment. The posthumous model for the Boer War Memorial in Warrington.

> No oaken coffin covered him,
> No Union Jack around him
> No loving wife to lay him out
> We buried him as we found him
>
> A thousand warriors round him
> Each with uncovered head
> Why does each man look sorrowful
> Our Gallant Leaders dead
>
> The Bravest of the Brave has gone
> You all have heard the story
> How a bullet laid him low
> Whilst leading us to glory

The scene of the South Lancashires' epic dash was captured by a participant and the painting has a proud position in the Museum at Preston.

The type of men involved is illustrated by a further and lighter story held by the Regiment. During the attack on Pieters Hill there was a soldier escorting a Boer prisoner and marching him down the hill.

'Boer: "I say, my man, I will give you my parole if you will only walk alongside of me; I wish to talk to you."

Lancashire. "Let me look at it first to see

how much it is worth." [no doubt he really said, 'lewk'!]

The Boer explained his word of honour.

Lancashire. "Oh is that all. Well never mind, I'm reet enough as I am," at the same time pushing the prisoner on.

Captive. "You had better be careful my man, I am a Field-Cornet."

Lancashire lad, scratching his head. "Si thee owd mon, I don't care if th'art a brass band tha'll hev to gooa in front!" Brandishing his bayonet, "Neaw, goo on!"'

According to Churchill the pragmatism of the burghers here asserted itself and while many retired to the laagers and the road north, many others fired as long as they could before throwing down their arms and surrendering. This is not to impute cowardice, however, because on Inniskilling the defenders were subjected to a massive barrage of shells and the hill-sides were alive with waiting infantrymen – but still the Boers held out. Now Major-General Norcott and the 4 Brigade joined in, the opportunity having come to reintroduce the naval guns. The whole strength of the Boers began to withdraw and a great convoy of horses and wagons moved north under observation from the military balloon. Buller apparently decided that mounted chase on a large scale was impossible, though many thought that persistence with his three military arms, following the methods recently perfected, could have crushed the Boer army in Natal.

A summary of events in the last push is made in this extract from General Sir Redvers Buller's despatch, 28th February 1900; -

'Finding that the passage of the Langverwacht Spruit was commanded by strong entrenchments I reconnoitred for another passage of the Tugela. One was found for me below the cataract by Colonel Sandbach RE.

On the 25th we commenced making an approach to it, and on the 26th, finding that I could make no practical approach, I crossed guns and baggage back to the south side of the Tugela, took up the pontoon bridge on the night of the 26th and relaid it at the new site, which is just below the point marked cataract. During all the time the troops had been scattered crouching under hastily constructed stone shelters and exposed to a galling shell and rifle fire, and throughout maintained the most excellent spirit. On the 27th General Barton with two battalions 6th Brigade and the Royal Dublin Fusiliers, crept about one and a half miles down the banks of the river, and ascending an almost precipitous cliff of about 500 ft assaulted and carried the top of Pieters Hill. This hill to a certain extent, turned the enemy's left,

An artist's impression of the Royal Lancasters carrying Pieters' Hill.

and the 4th Brigade, under Colonel Norcott and the 11th Brigade under Colonel Kitchener, the whole under General Warren, assailed the enemy's main position, which was magnificently carried by the South Lancashire Regiment about sunset. We took about 60 prisoners and scattered the enemy in all directions.

There seemed to be a considerable force of them left on and under Bulwana mountain. Our losses, I hope, are not large. They certainly are much less then they would have been were it not for the admirable manner in which the artillery was served, especially the guns mounted by the Royal Navy and the Natal Naval Volunteers.'

On the flat plain where stands Pieters Station, to the right the view is again framed by railway equipment and lineside furniture, but through the cables and their supports we can see the highest point of Pieters'. To the left the ground is also flatter and behind to the left reveals nothing of the terrors of the shambles below. The ground shows the same dishonesty as it did on the north side of Spion Kop, and, in fact, at the top of the Drakensberg – rolling and benign on one side and suddenly plunging and broken on the other.

149

Anyway, Buller had won – on the anniversary of Majuba.

The 28th revealed a manned balloon over Ladysmith, and to the 'aeronaut' was revealed the Boers in retreat, their big gun on Umbulwana silent and the road north behind it filled with horse-drawn traffic. The attackers now had the satisfaction of examining the empty trenches and vacated laagers on that comfortable slope behind them, greatly interested in the way their resolute adversaries had lived over the last four months. Fred Houghton of the York and Lancasters wrote to Mrs Houghton from Ladysmith on March 6th,

'Dead and wounded (were) lying in all directions. The Boer trenches were full. We buried all the dead next morning, burying the Boers in their own trenches. We also buried one of their women who had got killed. The enemy fled in all directions, leaving food, clothing, and ammunition behind, even bedsteads and tables. The General came round in the morning and we gave him a good cheer.'

Several observers remarked on the heaped clips of bullets conveniently at the defenders' feet. Many of them, as well as those discovered in caches, had had their tips removed so that they expanded on hitting bone, causing dreadful internal or exit injury.

By 1.00 p.m. White had heard that Buller had driven the Boers off the Tugela Line and they were retreating, while now it was noted that attempts were being made to remove 'Puffing Billy' from Umbulwana Hill. Since, at long last, it appeared that Buller was on his way, some of the precious 4.7″ ammunition was spent on hampering the work before a thunderstorm hid it.

Dundonald's men were feeling their way northwards, testing each rise in the ground for opposition and finding none. The enemy was truly evacuating the area, though their artillery was hanging on. As it was now early evening and the daylight was weakening, withdrawal back to the main body of the army seemed the correct course. However, at that point Major Hubert Gough [a controversial Army commander in the Great War], his forward scout, sent word that the road was at this minute clear all the way home, so Dundonald succumbed to the temptation to send the main body back, while he and Winston Churchill went forward to join Gough's party.

Gough would have none of it, however, and led the way over the Klip River, past Intombi Hospital and in to town. As the sun came out again they appeared to the defenders – 120 mounted infantry. They were welcomed in the town centre by Lieutenant-General Sir George White and the scout's brother, Captain John Gough, one of the

Mr and Mrs Wagner on Commando for three months at the Tugela Line. There are many instances of women serving with their husbands, from General P Joubert down to one sad lady whose mutilated remains were found on Pieter's Hill. The Natal Witness

garrison, was there to see him arrive.

So, at this moment, two famous brothers clasped hands. John, who won the VC in Somaliland in 1903 and who had reached the rank of Brigadier-General when he died of wounds in February 1915; and Hubert, who, as General Sir Hubert, was relieved of his command of the Fifth Army in March 1918. For eighteen years he was blamed for the massive loss of territory to the Germans in their great offensive of that month. Only in 1936 was he exonerated and awarded a KCB.

With typical English understatement Sergeant-Major Shaw, who had been immured throughout the siege, ended a letter to his cousin,

'The relief column arrived today amidst a scene of great enthusiasm. I must close to catch the post. Your affectionate cousin,

Walter Shaw.'

Ladysmith was relieved.

The Relief Force arrives.

The easy nature of the ground that was seen at the top of Pieters continues all the way to Ladysmith. Dundonald could not be sure what was in front of him that Wednesday evening; and the route also crosses undulations, but in a powered vehicle, on a metalled road they hold no hidden terrors. To the right, then to the left, the railway's wiry stripe smudges the brown and green, and now to the right industry is putting in an appearance with estates of mesh-bounded compounds dropped, as it were, on the veld. In front broods Umbulwana or Bulwana or another variant on the name, dominating the view. For now though, because the view is generally open, one can think how familiar and yet unfamiliar today's scene would be to the galloping Dundonald, Gough and Churchill, were they to ride across it again. The land is there, but the industry looks alien, and it has inevitably and properly brought with it workers. Unfortunately the victors of the war, Boer or British, forgot the workers so that now they are here many live in very poor conditions, often over the wire near the road. And they all, industrialists, workers and consumers alike have brought polythene – and left most of it on the roadside... From this side Umbulwana looming over the plastic somehow looks far less menacing than from the other, where Umbulwana is looming over the town.

And like Buller, you are now here, hopefully not to be described as Sir Redvers did his troops, 'a ragged-looking lot of ruffians they are, poor fellows, but fine men at that.'

Well, not the first bit.

Postscript

This is the end of your walking, and as the siege was now lifted, you could expect anticlimax. There was not, but there was still some way to go before the end of the tale, and sadness left to come for some of the senior British officers. For the Boer there was the long slog, increasingly bitter and at times, very successful, before, on May 31st 1902 he admitted defeat. For the gentleman in khaki ordered south, as Kipling jingoistically called him, there was more marching, more

General Sir Redvers Buller KCB, VC: Born 1839, 60th Rifles 1858, China 1860, Red River Expedition 1870, Ashanti War 1874, Kaffir War 1878, Zulu War 1878/79, Egypt 1882, Deputy Adjutant-General 1885, Under Secretary for Ireland 1887, Created the Army Service Corps 1888, Adjutant General 1890, Lieutenant-General 1891, General, and Commander at Aldershot 1898, Commander of Army Corps 1899. Superseded as Commander-in-Chief Lord Roberts. He died at Credition in 1908.

drinking of filthy water, more boring passages in dusty corners, more occasional murderous fusillades from mausers, more deaths of comrades from enteric fever, before he could go home.

Immediately there was the rest of Natal to clear – but Buller seemed to be in no rush. His detractors again found opportunity to gnaw at his reputation, yet Churchill, with all his own famous qualities and obvious faults, has the good-will to attribute Buller's delay to his concern for his troops. 1711 Private C. Chambers, 2nd West Yorkshires wrote on February 1st, 1900 with a similar view,

> '...General Buller is giving us a rest before he attacks again, and I think we shall be more successful next time. He is a noble man is Buller, and does not want condemning at all. If people could only see for themselves, they would think quite different. We are expecting to move every day now, and all the troops are cheerful and confident. You would not know me now with having whiskers on. I look a beauty. Ellison [remember his comments on being under shell-fire, page 94], out of Silver-street, [sic] was wounded the day before I arrived.'

2868 Private Jaques of 'F' Company, 1st York and Lancaster Regiment, said on February 18th:

> 'the next morning we had General Sir R. Buller, and he came and spoke to us, and he did feel for us. You could hear the General asking the men if they could eat their food... A few words about General Buller. In the first place I think myself he is a very clever man, and knows his duty, but I am very sorry to say he has had some hard lines, and by what I have seen in the English papers they do not seem to give him much credit for what he has done. For myself I give him great credit, and I would follow him anywhere, even if death stared me in the face...'

That affection for his men never left him, and if the correspondents quoted above were typical, the men reciprocated in full measure. These writers were northerners with no civilian connection to the Devon landowner whatsoever and writing to a northern newspaper at that, but men from all over the country felt the same. At the end, in 1908, when his peers had left him, metaphorically speaking, his Old Comrades in the Other Ranks stood by him, and whether they heard of the epitaph on the statue erected in Exeter or not, they agreed with it –"He Saved Natal" – with their help, of course.

They loved and respected him to the grave.

On March 2nd it was reckoned that it would need a month before the garrison of Ladysmith would be fit for service, and re-equipping was required to the extent that the cavalry had no more than two hundred horses, and those nearly useless.

The 2000 patients at Intombi, in a 'deplorable condition,' said *The Times History of the War*, needed to be moved south and this could only be done at the rate of about one hundred a day by rail, a facility which was concentrating on the priority of northbound traffic with supplies for Ladysmith. It took until the 27th of the month to move the unfortunates to various better hospitals in Natal.

Other changes were effected and on the 9th of March General Sir C. Warren of Spion Kop fame (or infamy) left for a new post in the Cape; as did Major-General I. Hamilton, later in charge at Gallipoli in 1915, Colonel Sir H. S. Rawlinson and others en route for posts with Lord Roberts. Rawlinson, like Hamilton, had Great War fame and in 1918 led with great distinction in the weeks before the armistice. However, the 59,000 casualties on the Somme on 1st July, 1916 will forever be associated with his name for he was the unsuccessful commander of the Fourth Army that sustained them.

The enemy, meanwhile, had raised the siege, but they had not moved far and by the middle of the month they had established a line stretching from the Cundycleugh Pass in the west as far as Helpmekaar in the east. (Helpmekaar had been a supply base for Lord Chelmsford's attack on Cetshwayo in 1879 and the main supply for Rorke's Drift.) Control of the Cundycleugh in the Drakensberg also gave the Boers charge of the mountains as far down as Van Reenan's pass. They now had, it was thought, some 16000 men with 30 guns, but by the end of the month the drain on their strength occasioned by the reinforcing of the Orange Free State area had reduced them to six or seven thousand.

By April 20th Elandslaagte, which had been the scene of the bitter fight in the previous October, was part of Hildyard's defence line, he now being in charge of the Vth Division instead of General C. Warren.

Buller had previously had the idea of pushing westward through the Tintwa, Van Reenan's and Bezuidenhout passes but Lord Roberts was against the plan, believing that the Natal Field Force should remain on the defensive. Early in May he changed his mind and told Buller to 'Occupy the enemy's attention on the Biggarsberg, and, as their numbers decrease... move your troops towards the Transvaal repairing the railway as you advance.'

It all moved quickly now and the carping at 'Sir Reverse' Buller was stilled.

He directed Hildyard up the Dundee road and railway, and Clery round via Helpmekaar to Dundee, which was re-occupied on May

15th. By the 17th the mounted troops were at Newcastle and Dundonald was reconnoitring the position at Laing's Nek on the 19th, where the Boers were in strength: they had guns placed from Majuba Hill across the road eastward with a 6″ Creusot at the end. Hildyard continued along the railway line which was repaired so as to serve as the main supply route.

On 30th May Buller attempted to discuss the possibility of the enemy's surrender but the Boer leader told him that he had to report to his Government, who, it transpired, would not agree to the idea. He used three days however to improve his positions, before rejecting Buller's suggestions, but Sir Redvers also worked hard during the 'rest' and on 6th June he controlled the southern approach to Botha's Pass.

Hubert Gough, then a major, later a Lieutenant General who was relieved of his command in France in 1918.

John Gough, then a captain, won the VC in Somaliland in 1903, died of wounds in France in 1915, when a Brigadier-General.

On 6th June he sent the South African Light Horse against the Boers at Van Wyk's Hill, thereafter making for the Spitz Kop and adjacent hills where the enemy were irregularly positioned in trenches with Vickers-Maxims, two field guns, and a 6″ Creusot east of Laing's Nek and Majuba. They attempted to take back Van Wyke's but Talbot Coke had strengthened it and the 2nd Royal Lancasters had hauled up two 4.7″ guns and two 12 pounders so that the Boers were forced off the pass.

On 8th June the South African Light Horse occupied Spitz Kop and the 11th and 2nd Brigades passed on each side, driving the Boers back onto the crest of the Berg, the opposition fading by 4.00 pm with the Boers retreating behind 'hundreds of acres of flaming grass'. Two men were killed, one officer and twelve men were wounded.

Buller now needed to force Alleman's Nek which had only recently been occupied by the Boers and therefore, Buller reasoned, could not yet be entrenched. It can be seen on the map that the British thus looped west and north on top of the Drakensberg, leaving Majuba Hill and the area about it side-stepped. On the 11th with the cavalry on each wing and South African Light Horse as a rearguard they encountered a field gun and two Vickers-Maxims again, which the Royal Horse Artillery countered, along with howitzers. At 2.00 p.m. further big guns arrived and the enemy were quietened, and at 2.30 the infantry advanced across approximately two and a half miles of open grass, with no cover, which was dominated by the nek and by two small kopjes lined by riflemen of the Carolina and Lydenburg Commandos, with Johannesburg, Pretoria, Zoutpansberg and Swaziland Police being represented.

Hildyard was in charge as the southern kop was attacked by 2nd Dorsets and 1st Royal Dublin Fusiliers with the 2nd Middlesex in support, and on the north side were the 2nd Queens and the 2nd East Surreys with the 2nd West Yorks at the rear.

The Dorsets were on the main crest-line by 5.00 pm after co-ordinated artillery and infantry work. 19 were killed and 123 wounded, four of whom died from their wounds.

That night the Boers knew that they were outflanked on Laing's Nek and they retired from the whole area so that the next day, 12th June 1900, they were driven out of Natal.

What a difference four months can make. The conclusion of the Invasion of Natal had been reached, but, in a way, the story began and finished around Ladysmith.

And in the end, who won? Who really won? Not the British. Not the Boers. Could it be that now, in the 1990s the silent and largely unreported sufferers in the war, the coloured and black Africans have won?

We still do not know – not for sure.

INDEX

158